Seeking Faith
Finding God

Seeking Faith
Finding God

Getting to grips with questions of faith

John Rackley

Text copyright © John Rackley 2007
The author asserts the moral right
to be identified as the author of this work

Published by
The Bible Reading Fellowship
First Floor, Elsfield Hall
15–17 Elsfield Way, Oxford OX2 8FG
Website: www.brf.org.uk

ISBN 978 1 84101 543 9
First published 2007
10 9 8 7 6 5 4 3 2 1 0
All rights reserved

Acknowledgments
Unless otherwise stated, scripture quotations are taken from The New Revised
Standard Version of the Bible, Anglicized Edition, copyright © 1989, 1995 by the
Division of Christian Education of the National Council of the Churches of Christ in
the USA, and are used by permission. All rights reserved.

Scripture quotations taken from the Holy Bible, New International Version, copyright
© 1973, 1978, 1984 by International Bible Society, are used by permission of
Hodder & Stoughton Limited. All rights reserved. 'NIV' is a registered trademark of
International Bible Society. UK trademark number 1448790.

A catalogue record for this book is available from the British Library

Printed in Singapore by Craft Print International Ltd

Contents

Introduction

This series of reflections began as a column in *The Baptist Times*. The editor at that time, Hazel Southam, suggested I write material that would encourage readers to look at their Bible with fresh eyes. This I sought to do—and I leave it to the reader to say whether I have achieved this goal!

In this selection, I am following that original aim. I also wish to explore what it means to be a disciple of Jesus, living according to his gospel today. I aim to go 'behind the scenes' to consider the struggles and hopes of being Christian in the 21st century.

Recent conversations at our church in Bath revealed that many of us are very timid when it comes to sharing our faith. Reasons given were lack of understanding and erosion of confidence. We feel that popular culture offers such a poor image of the Church that we are beaten before we start. The result is that there is a profound ignorance of the gospel in our culture and many people live with a parody of what it means to be a Christian.

The gospel, however, expects us to communicate what we believe with a view to convincing others of its authenticity. I believe this begins to happen when Christian people are ready to have seeking and searching faith themselves. If we are to communicate what we believe, it must be as fellow travellers in these difficult and demanding times. Hence my first selection of reflections in this book speaks of 'a yearning faith'. To live with faith in God means that we live with a longing to know him and discover more about his purpose. Our faith seeks to know God more deeply because it is a faith founded on love for God, a love that absorbs our whole being.

This seeking faith of ours is not without guidance or purpose, however. 'A gospel place' and 'Gospel encounters' investigate the life and times of Jesus, as knowing him—which includes knowing about him—is a core part of what it means to be seeking God and finding faith. Occasionally I slip out of his century into our own, for 'gospel encounters' are always happening.

One of the joys of this journey of discovery is the encounter with the community of faith that surrounds us as we make our way. 'Faith companions' describes some of my experiences. They are of necessity personal but I offer them in a spirit of gratitude for those who have shared their journey with me.

'Praying the gospel' takes us to what we call the Lord's Prayer. These words have sustained the worship and work of Christian people throughout the story of the Church. They are a remarkable testimony to the faith of Jesus and his relationship with God. I do not believe we can be closer to the heart of Christ than when we pray the prayer with trust and hope.

You will discover that I insert a 'link' between sections. This serves two purposes. It offers the route my thinking is taking as I move to the next part and gives some idea of what the new section is about. It also serves as a reminder that what I am writing is like my weekly *Baptist Times* column: it is 'work in progress'. I believe in a theology of the journey. I cannot find it in myself to write an ordered, systematic account of what I believe. I am constantly working at it, and do not fear going to the edge of my beliefs, raising questions and exploring new ideas.

There are a number of imagination-led reflections in this book. The creation of imaginary thoughts from characters in the Gospels can only be a speculative task, and I am aware that such thoughts come from my own subjective research into the texts and the present reality of my belief in the meaning of the cross and resurrection. Yet I seek to honour that subjectivity without casting it in certainty. When I contemplate the characters concerned, I give them more room than the Gospel writers did. I wish they could speak for themselves! What would you have them say?

I thank Mary, my wife, for her support throughout this enterprise, letting me 'disappear into my head' as another idea arises! I also thank the people of Manvers Street Baptist Church who have heard these ideas over the years and helped me develop them, and also Mark Woods, the present editor of *The Baptist Times*, who encouraged me to turn my weekly 'Rackley's Reflections' into what I now offer here.

A yearning faith

Seeking God

For God alone my soul waits in silence;
from him comes my salvation.
PSALM 62:1

There was an old lay preacher who used to take me to task when I began a service with the words 'Let us worship God'. He would ask, 'What would you say if someone called out "No" or "I'm not ready yet"?'

I told him they should arrive early to prepare themselves or, like the 19th-century Baptists used to do in my home town of Brixham in Devon, meet for a preparatory prayer meeting on the previous Saturday night. He was not impressed with my answer. He followed his own counsel and, when he led worship, would say, 'Let us seek God together.'

I have grown to appreciate what this preacher meant. He was not belittling the call to worship; he was just allowing the experience to be human. I thought of his sensitivity as I led worship during the weekend that the awful tragedy of Beslan unfolded. The indescribable horror of schoolchildren being held hostage by bomb-wearing terrorists filled my mind as I came to the church and changed what I had planned for the service.

It had happened to me before. Both the 1989 Hillsborough disaster in Sheffield and the death of Princess Diana in 1997 had happened less than 24 hours before a Sunday morning service, and I could not ignore what was on everyone's mind on those occasions. There were so many questions reminding us of our own 'whys' and 'what nows'. The start of a service cannot disregard the people who are seeking to worship God.

So, on that Sunday morning in September 2004, the flood of images from North Ossetia arrived in that service, imprinted on the minds and hearts of the worshippers. Russia was experiencing its own 9/11 and the questions came: 'Why does God let such things happen? What drives people to commit such crimes? Can we offer Russia total support when its government's policies may have been part of the reason for the tragedy? What is the gospel word that needs to be heard in the space created by our time together?'

I have been the minister of Manvers Street Baptist Church for a long time. We have been through much together. There before me were people of courage, faith, anguish, fear, stubbornness, doubt, frustration, anger and joy—all there ready to use Christian words of faith and hope. This Sunday found us together, seeking to collect the offering of the week and bring it to the Lord's table in worship. I am constantly amazed that some still turn up, for they have so much in their lives that could have turned them away from God. It's the mystery of worship.

With all that goes on in our lives, I would have understood if someone had said on that day, 'Wait! Are we ready for this? Are we ready to worship with all that's gone on this week in our life, and what's going on now in Beslan?'

Of course, some will say that the focus of worship is God, not us. We step away for a time from the headlines and demands of life and see beyond the immediate—the fallen world and all its fatal attraction. Correct: there is a place for humility in worship. We gather in the presence of the mystery that is God, to celebrate the discovery of the revelation of his nature in Christ. But this gathering should not be an anaesthetic that clouds judgment or deadens feeling. Worship of God does not remove us from this world, but it helps us to see the world differently.

The psalms of yearning combine anguished human questioning with faithful seeking of God in situations that appear to be incomprehensible. The seeking is part of the worship. We all seek God. We should not let the discovery of his grace and the action of his Spirit in our lives make us complacent. Paul, writing to the Colossians, implores them to look for the things that are above, the life that is hidden in Christ, yet he grounds it in the difficult reality of a morally ambiguous culture (Colossians 3:1–11).

An old hymn says, 'I sought the Lord, and afterward I knew He moved my soul to seek Him, seeking me' (Anon., c.1880). The anguished cries of the psalmists, as they pour out regret, terror and puzzlement in the light of events, seek the seeking God. Faith can scream 'Why?' while believing that the Lord longs to offer us yet more light, and that truth will break forth from his word.

God is like a shepherd passionately committed to finding the sheep lost from his flock, but, for us, that experience may often be like an anguished searching, knocking at a door that won't open simply at our bidding (Matthew 7:7–11). When Jesus spoke those words in Matthew 7, he was encouraging a seeking, exploring faith on the assumption that God will not play with us. God is like a generous parent, but is not at our beck and call.

At the heart of faith there is a yearning—a yearning that is not about having questions answered or doubts removed but rather having a desire to know God and his will. This longing is not the preserve of the specially gifted or those with time for 'that sort of thing'. It is the blessing that Jesus described at the beginning of the Sermon on the Mount as poverty of spirit and a hunger for righteousness (Matthew 5:3, 6). With that blessing, we can live as both seekers and disciples, for they are both one and the same.

For reflection

Read Psalms 5, 27, 42, 43 and 63.

Prayer suggestion

Offer God your own honest longings without fear or self-censorship.

For discussion

What experiences have most tested your faith or made you seek God more deeply?

The sanctity of struggle

'You have striven with God and with humans, and have prevailed.'
GENESIS 32:28

Within the space of one afternoon, two people facing strange and difficult times asked me two very similar questions: 'Why do I get no answers when I ask God questions?' and 'Do you think, when I get to meet him in heaven, I'll get some personal attention?'

Many people struggle with God. This is not the same as struggling to believe whether God exists or not. It is the discovery that a relationship with God can be unnerving and demanding. I do not wish to disparage people for whom faith comes out of a clear blue sky and is a source of deep consolation. This is a gift of grace, for which we can give God the glory. For many, however, it is their belief in God that makes him most puzzling.

I call it the 'Jacob experience'. Jacob's story spans half of Genesis. He was a quiet man, a mother's favourite and the cause of a father's heartbreak. He had an uneasy relationship with his elder brother and eventually became estranged from him. Years of exile followed. Meanwhile, God is in the background as a shadowy presence who opens and closes wombs, gives dreams and receives prayer. Jacob's prayers are a mixture of humility and bargaining. He has a troubled relationship with God.

Eventually, in Genesis 32:22–31, there is an episode that has taken on an iconic significance. The struggle of Jacob with a stranger at Jabbock river has become, for many, a metaphor of their relationship with God.

Jacob has denied himself human companionship. He waits at

night in solitude, at a place of transition. He is a man who has struggled with himself and others. The God who has been hidden in the twists and turns of his experience emerges from the darkness of the night, and a fight begins that will leave Jacob changed for good, with an injury and a new name. We are told that Jacob fought a man, but he believes he has survived a bruising encounter with God.

It is obvious from the way the story is told that it presented difficulties to the editors of Genesis. They could see various meanings in the event, and the ambiguity is important. There is something rather primitive going on.

Jacob is no pristine holy man. His encounter with God is brutal, raw and complex. To tidy up its meaning is to miss the point. An experience of spiritual depth can be wounding. We can never go back and be the kind of person we were before. The wound may not cripple us but it acts as a constant reminder of the struggle and the closeness of failure. Jacob discovered his own poverty of spirit and received a blessing—a sublime paradox!

Times of turbulence bring their own gift to our faith. A river may move from a calm stretch into rapids as it descends through a gorge. Yet it is in the rapids that a canoeist discovers more about the river and develops the skill and trust to cope with the experience. Once in the racing river, it is very difficult to get out. There is no returning to the point of departure and the experience has to be both accepted and endured. The water is both friend and foe.

The letter to the Hebrews tells us that Jesus, 'the pioneer and perfecter of our faith... for the sake of the joy that was set before him endured the cross' (Hebrews 12:2). Our Lord accepted the necessity of his sacrifice, but it was no easy experience. His Gethsemane struggles were taken into the cross, where their questioning and fear became part of his offering to the Father. This is the way of sacred struggle.

To journey with Jesus means that we will know his risen presence as much through times of despair, grief and disappointment as in experiences of delight. To believe in God is to feel passionately the meaninglessness of life when it overwhelms us or others. This sensitivity is given with the gift of faith. Faith in God brings with it an experience of how God himself experiences his wayward world— although, through his grace, we are shielded from the full bitter impact. Our Lord bore that for us: for him there was no anaesthetic to obliterate the pain. Now, together, we struggle for the transformation of our world.

For reflection

Read Isaiah 52:13—53:12.

Prayer suggestion

Offer your own experience of struggle to God and ask that he will let good emerge through what you have faced.

For discussion

Who has inspired you by the way in which they have struggled in their faith and overcome the difficulties?

Living the question

In John's Gospel, Thomas has the role of the questioning disciple. On two occasions he enables Jesus to reveal more than was being seen at the time.

First, in John 14:5, Thomas speaks with characteristic bluntness. Jesus has spoken of going on a journey of preparation, and Thomas is very direct in his response. He speaks for all the disciples: 'We do not know where you are going. How can we know the way there?' Jesus, in his reply, reveals a truth that will hold for all time: he is the way to God the Father, the path to life in all its fullness. Thomas' question preceded the answer. Without the question, the answer could not have been given at that time.

In John 20, Thomas is once again the questioner. He has missed the first resurrection appearance of Jesus to the disciples, and he is not going to base any future hope on hearsay. He wants a personal audience just for himself. He is expecting personal contact and ample evidence that Jesus is the one who is giving the other disciples such reassurance. He expects to see scars; he needs to touch the woundedness of Christ. It is the marks of crucifixion on the resurrection body of Jesus that will convince him.

What is Thomas really asking for? I think Thomas needed to know that what had happened throughout the life of Jesus, which had ended so awfully on the cross, had not been left behind. He needed to know that everything he and the other disciples had gone though with Jesus would be part of its meaning. His questions were part of his relationship with Christ, and they would shape his future as a follower of Jesus.

Once again, the questions set up what Jesus needed to say to his disciples. For Jesus, the signs of his crucifixion on his risen body would tell their own story. He had told the disciples that, just as the Father had sent him, so they too were being sent, as part of God's mission of love to save a world in danger of perishing. But this mission had left its mark on his Son, so they should expect nothing different. To be engaged in God's mission can leave us vulnerable and hurt.

It was Thomas' uncertainty that paved the way for the response of Jesus. But then Jesus tells Thomas to stop doubting and believe (20:27). Jesus is inviting Thomas to move on. He provides the evidence that Thomas needs and expects it to release Thomas from his doubts. The questions and doubts had taken the disciple so far, but now he could go no further with them.

Doubt has its value: it questions; it explores; it refuses to accept answers that have no cost. It presses the 'pause' button and waits for matters to unfold. I fear, however, that some people develop a doubt syndrome. They have a question or a doubt to which they seek an answer. It nags away, and they feel they cannot move on in their faith unless it is resolved. It looms over them like a threatening thunderstorm that never actually breaks, but paralyses by its presence. In the end, the doubt becomes a block to any sort of change.

Sometimes faith has to say that the questions do not have answers and what we are called to do is live the questions. The questions become what our faith is about. This is what we have to offer God and this is what he receives.

In the Gospel of John, Jesus provokes faith and doubt, which both question. First come the disciples of John the Baptist (1:35–42); then Nicodemus approaches Jesus at night with a question and leaves puzzled (3:4–10). A Samaritan woman challenges Jesus with her convictions and discovers that their conversation raises a fundamental question for her (4:29). The questions continue to flow from religious leaders, foreign pilgrims, Annas the high priest and Pilate, until we come to a question of Jesus himself to Mary Magdalene (John 20:15). God revealed his Son through the questioning he raised in the lives of the people around him.

There are also times to doubt the doubts and to challenge their power and importance. At those times, it can be helpful to place them in a wider context than their own terms of reference. In this way, the power of doubt is used against itself. This is what Jesus offered Thomas. His discipleship did not need to be only about his questions.

As Jesus addresses the needs of Thomas, it is as if he looks over Thomas' shoulder and sees many others—the beginning of a long line of questioners and doubters, who still seek to know the Saviour. Jesus tells Thomas that he is fortunate: he has had the opportunity to believe the evidence of his own eyes. But those who believe without seeing the body of the risen Christ are also blessed.

I wonder what Thomas thought of what Jesus said. Did he see the responsibility that Jesus was placing on his and the other disciples' shoulders? It was the responsibility of providing an opportunity for others to come to Christ through the witness of those who were already his followers—a witness that would make it possible to believe without the evidence in view.

Questioners can feel threatening in the life of a church. They will often seem out of step. They talk about issues that others do not wish to address. They refuse to be silent when others are opting for a quiet life. Some, like Thomas, challenge the experience of others and can sound very awkward. Sometimes the questions are fed by hurt or the need for more information. Sometimes, as in the case of Thomas, the questioner is not yet in the right place to receive the answer.

The questions may burden the questioner, yet they may be an opening for the work of God to continue. They may hold the key to release under the guidance of the Holy Spirit.

For reflection

Read John 18:1–38 and track the questions through to Pilate's final yearning plea.

Prayer suggestion

Offer to God your own questioning as a way of being used in his service.

For discussion

In your experience, how well does your church cope with those who raise questions that unsettle others?

Unfinished symphonies

Jesus said to Mary, 'Do not hold on to me.'
JOHN 20:17

A somewhat jaundiced friend told me that our children are born to disappoint us. We dream dreams for them that they cannot fulfil, and when they grow up, their parents disappoint them in turn. This friend was too downbeat for me! The fact that he was saying this at his daughter's wedding made it even more poignant. What had happened over the years to make him sound so disappointed and disillusioned?

It is true, however, that we do create expectations that we cannot deliver. Wedding services can be too full of them. I have real reservations about what people expect from marriage. It is a wonderful gift, but I am sure that no one relationship can deliver everything we need. If we are not careful, we awaken one day and realize we are still dreaming dreams for ourselves that will never become a reality.

It has been described as the discovery that in this life 'all symphonies are unfinished' (see Ronald Rolheiser, *Seeking Spirituality*, Hodder & Stoughton, 1998). From the moment we begin to live in this multi-choice world, we hope for, plan and desire far more than we will achieve. We start more than we complete, and what we believe we have completed, another will dismantle and assemble differently.

This is the experience of sharing the nature of the Creator. We live in a universe of infinite potential where countless symphonies will be begun. They will have their time and then be left behind. Research of all types is only just beginning to discover the outskirts of creation's glory. The image of God in us, though tarnished and off-course, makes us reach out for fulfilment and long for achievement. This is what makes the ageing process so challenging. We sense our world shrinking as our physical capacity becomes more limited, but often the desire to go beyond that capacity is still strong. So begins a tussle and tension that may never be resolved.

Mary Magdalene was delighted to discover that Jesus was with her again. She clung to him. This time there would be no letting go. Yet, for her, his resurrection brought a moment of painful discovery: what he had been, he no longer was. There had been an ending; now there was a beginning—a beginning that meant she could not have an exclusive claim on him. She was now part of a picture bigger than she could ever have imagined. Her relationship with Jesus had become absorbed into his future, in which he would go to the Father and complete all that was incomplete. What seemed to have ended incomplete was, in fact, part of something more. Unfinished symphonies carry within them the seeds of the next.

When we have children, we have far too many best wishes for them. When we get married, we have far too many expectations. When we begin a new job, move to a new place, move to another church or take retirement, we are starting symphonies that will be, in the end, incomplete.

There is no point trying to stop the hopes, desires and plans, but there is very much point in letting them go when their time is past. The skill is in doing this in a way that does not make us bitter because they do not seem to have reached completion. It requires us to recognize that we have a desire for fulfilment that nothing or no one in this life can make complete.

The gift of hope, seeing possibilities and dreaming dreams, is what it means to be 'a little lower than God' (Psalm 8:5). There is a sacred trust between humankind and the Creator in which we accept the duty to be careful stewards of not only the resources of the earth but also the harvest of our experience, gifts and dreams. The trust between the Creator and ourselves will mean that we also experience the pain of the Creator—the pain of watching gifts being thrown away unused and seeing the symphonies that have never begun. There is also the pain of watching a person cling on when the symphony has moved to another theme.

Mary needed to discover that letting go is a journey toward life. It is therefore, in the light of the resurrection, a journey toward a tomb. There, the old life is enfolded so that a new one can grow. The faith of Easter realizes that there is no life without the losing of life. In the tomb of our incompleteness, another life begins to emerge that takes us to a different place. This transition will not be easy. We can hold on to cherished hopes long after there is any realistic hope that they will be fulfilled, thus building up regret and resentment. We can find ourselves looking back over our life, marking certain times with an 'if only'. We may find that the only way we can cope is to blame another person or set of circumstances, and shun them.

Letting go will start an argument within ourselves over how much we wish the change to happen—an argument between all that wants to hold on and all that wants to advance. It is a discovery within us of the freedom to choose; when we discover that freedom, we can begin to clear away our attachment to what is incomplete and un-finished, until we get down to the core, which is the fullness of life that Jesus described as the reason for his coming (John 10:10).

When the clearing process begins, we start being less concerned about what we are letting go and more focused on what will give life to ourselves or others. This is, perhaps, the unexpected cost of Easter living.

For reflection

Read Colossians 3:1–14. What symphonies does Paul expect us to conclude?

Prayer suggestion

Seek strength from God to release you from anything you are not prepared to let go, which may be draining you of life.

For discussion

What ways have you discovered of making 'letting go' easier?

A time of seeking

'Where is the child who has been born king of the Jews?'
MATTHEW 2:2

I regret that the nativity stories of the Gospels have become exclusively linked to the season of Christmas. So, somewhat perversely, I try to take the opportunity to preach on the story of the magi at other times of the year. I have been pleased to find this approach both refreshing and applauded by members of my congregation.

The story of the travellers who made their way to Jerusalem seeking a king has become part of the mythology of Christmas. When I use the word 'mythology', I am not questioning whether such an event actually occurred. I am suggesting that the story has taken on the power of myth: it has become a core feature of the meaning of Christmas, and is also a parable for our day and age. I think, perhaps, it should be introduced with the words 'Once upon a time...' because, as we know, stories that begin that way have an appeal far beyond an account of something that may or may not have happened. Stories like that capture hearts and minds with a powerful attraction. They mirror our own desires and longings. We recognize ourselves in them.

In countless nativity plays, the arrival of the strangers from the east is depicted as a splendid, colourful climax to the welcome for Jesus, the Saviour of the world. They bow in humble obedience and offer the gifts of their lives to the other little stranger whom they have travelled so far to meet. Yet Matthew did not intend this beginning of his version of the Gospel to be part of a nativity play. He wrote it to explain who Jesus is and who can become his followers.

In his book, *Do Christians Know How to be Spiritual?* (DLT, 2005), John Drane raises this rather disconcerting question because he wants to explore why our age of spiritual hunger and inquisitiveness does not bring people to our churches. He suggests that the words 'church' and 'spiritual searcher' can no longer be put together, and creates a convincing argument that those who are exploring their spiritual nature do not think the Church has anything to offer. He proposes that if we are to convince them otherwise, we need to become radically different.

I found myself by turns fascinated, puzzled, upset, chastened and challenged by this suggestion. I know there are spiritual searchers in our churches and wish there were more. I know we can come across to our timid, religion-averse contemporaries as too full of our certainties. We no longer seek to find because we believe we have the answer; yet, paradoxically, this belief has created a sort of depression that makes it very difficult for us to speak naturally and openly about our relationship with God. I also know that when we create spaces of common ground where believer and agnostic seek the face of God together, great and wonderful things happen.

John Drane is right. Too often, when people come to our churches asking whether we know the way to Jesus, we can act rather like King Herod. We can feel threatened and put on the spot, and we send for the minister! I fear that too many of us have lost the will and the capacity to witness to our personal faith in the Lord. In this age of spiritual searching, people ask questions that either surprise or disarm us, and we feel ill-equipped to respond.

Matthew would be surprised that this is happening. He would be surprised that so much energy is spent on trying to work out whether or not there was a star over Bethlehem, because he was writing for the sake of the very people who are not coming to churches these days.

Near the beginning of his Gospel, Matthew introduces us to the magi. The word means 'magician', and refers to those who were experts in interpreting dreams and strange happenings, especially by means of stargazing and astrology. There was nothing royal about these men, although they would appear to have been wealthy. More importantly, they were on a journey of discovery. They sought the king of the Jews, and what Matthew is saying in this story is that even though Jesus was the king of the Jews, his rule was not limited to the Jews because even pagan star-readers wanted to worship him.

This is exactly what had been expected by the prophets of Israel. At the heart of their prophecies about the coming king, the Messiah, is the belief that he would bring God's rule of justice and peace to all peoples (see Psalm 72; Isaiah 11:1–10). This was what upset Herod when the magi asked him to show them the king of the Jews. The birth of this child-king was not only a threat to his dynasty. It would be a challenge to Rome, the dominant empire of that time, introducing a completely new authority into the checks and balances of Jewish/Roman politics.

At the beginning of his Gospel, Matthew encourages all spiritual searchers to come to Jesus. He asks us to listen to the story of Jesus and consider his links to the hopes of previous generations. He encourages us to treat Jesus inclusively, as God's Messiah for everyone, and invites us to come to him by whatever route we can, to offer him whatever we have to give. The worldwide mission of Jesus' followers is to bring others to heaven by trust in Jesus. There is no bar on the basis of culture, history or religion, for all are welcome in the kingdom of God (Matthew 28:18–20).

We live in a time of spiritual searchers and, as Christians, we need to take our place among them. We need to be humble enough to acknowledge that although we know 'the Way', we haven't arrived at our destination. Jesus himself lived among such spiritual seekers and his Spirit in us will lead us to encounters like his in our mission as his disciples. When we forget this, we become like Herod and his court theologians, defensive in our certainties and protective of our self-interest.

Bethlehem was a place that didn't count for much, yet it became the birthplace of God's glory on earth. Perhaps a church of spiritual searchers needs to be more like Bethlehem—a hamlet among the fields—and less like the walled city of Jerusalem.

For reflection

Read Matthew 2:1–12 and its sequel, Matthew 28:16–20.

Prayer suggestion

For one week, at least three times in each day, pause and read slowly the Beatitudes (Matthew 5:3–12) as a prayer of thanksgiving.

For discussion

Do you think there is enough spiritual seeking in the life of the Church?

Faith in imagination

Jesus said: 'Look at the birds of the air; they neither sow nor reap nor gather into barns, and yet your heavenly Father feeds them. Are you not of more value than they?'
MATTHEW 6:26

One Advent, I travelled to Scargill House in North Yorkshire to lead a retreat with a friend of many years, Ron Ayres. We met with people from different Christian traditions, times of life and experience.

Ron and I had decided that as the Common Lectionary was using the Gospel of Mark for its readings the coming year, we would concentrate on that Gospel for the duration of the retreat. It soon became apparent that Mark was totally suited to the bluff hills of the Dales and for a company of people who were immersed in snow, bitter winds and horizontal rain for much of the time. Like the Gospel itself, however, we started on a bright, clear blue sky morning with only a hint of the storms to come.

What we did over the space of three days was simply to read the Gospel with as little commentary as necessary. We wanted the text to speak for itself. We aimed to let it reach the hearts and minds of us all without censor or obligation. There was no 'authorized' interpretation in sight save how Ron and I and others chose to read. Occasionally we would read a story through, then slowly pause to consider its differing features and and watch the to-and-fro of each moment in the account. The events of Gethsemane were remembered in Scargill's walled garden and the final puzzling words of the Gospel were read with our bags packed, ready to return to our 'Galilees' with the Lord travelling ahead of us.

To do this sort of thing is not easy for me. Any study of biblical interpretation that I do is heavily dependent on my commentaries and the insights of current historical research into the person of Jesus and first-century Galilee. I still use the sort of research that explores the original language of the text—who might have written it and why, and why the Gospel writers change details and the order in which they record events. I am sure I do not use these tools well or consistently, but I do remember my New Testament tutor warning us to read the text before the commentaries (although my tutor would have preferred me to read the text in Greek).

Now I am finding that I just let the scripture speak for itself and notice its effect on me. I am placing far more trust in the gift of imagination. That will sound dangerous to some people. Imagination can lead us down all sorts of misleading paths. When it comes to scripture, imagination must be tempered by the gifts of those who know the language and context of what is being read. Here, however, are some of my discoveries about Mark's Gospel from our reading at Scargill:

- Discipleship is about faith that questions and struggles with the call to trust God when everything seems strange and against common sense (Mark 4:35–41; 8:31–37). Jesus puzzles us with his challenges to conventional thinking.
- Jesus commends those who responded to him, for the part that their faith plays. He applauds faith that has done well (Mark 5:34; 10:52). On the other hand, he never speaks of having faith in him. Jesus is one who provokes faith into life, and in his company we discover the disposition to life that we call faith.
- On reading Mark 9:33—10:45, one of the few sequences of Jesus' teaching contained in the Gospel, I became angry at the isolating incomprehension of the disciples. Jesus was trying to lay out the values of the kingdom of God and met reactions that must have driven him to despair. By contrast, when I came to Mark 13 with its dire warnings, I felt that they were spoken from the pastoral heart of Jesus, who could see what a difficult and demanding time lay in wait for his followers.

- Jesus' question to Bartimaeus, 'What do you want me to do for you?' (Mark 10:51), felt almost like a signing-off. Jesus would shortly be surrounded by the turmoil of his final week, with little time for those who needed his healing. The question echoes through that last week of his life as we watch him becoming increasingly immersed in the duplicity and lack of understanding of his accusers.
- I read the account of Jesus' last moments before the black wrought-iron cross in Scargill's chapel. His last cry became one of desperate puzzlement. He was prepared for the isolation resulting from the actions of his enemies and his followers, but not for the abandonment by God his Father (Mark 15:34). This is the deep point of the covenant made in his blood. It is not the place to argue over atonement theory. The emotional impact of Jesus' cry reveals that he lived the faith he encouraged in others.

I do not claim any originality in these discoveries, but they came to me by letting the Gospel of Mark speak for itself.

In the hymn 'Break thou the bread of life' by Mary Lathbury, we find the line 'Beyond the sacred page I seek thee, Lord.' I think the writer was celebrating something very important here: the Lord revealed in scripture is the Lord *of* scripture.

When we read the Bible, it is necessary to understand what we read. We might wish to discover as much as we can about the writers and the context in which they were writing. We can start a fascinating exploration when we examine the various levels of development undertaken by many of our scripture texts. In the final analysis, however, reading scripture is about an encounter. We do not read the Bible for itself but for the one whom the Bible reveals. This is where faith in imagination is important.

Jesus used his imagination to create his parables. They might have been about the everyday world of his listeners, but no one before had connected their observation of that world with an apprehension of what God was doing. Jesus brought together what had previously been kept separate. Through faith in imagination, he was able to reveal what had been hidden by making unexpected links and correlations. So a merchant's pearl and hidden treasure in a field, a woman searching for a coin and a harvest of weeds among the corn all became signs of the way and work of God.

When Jesus asked the crowds on the hillside to consider the feeding habits of birds as the handiwork of God, he was expecting them to use their imaginations, not conduct a scientific enquiry. Jesus was a person of imagination. He did not make up what he said, but what he said was informed by what he saw going on. What he saw was always the work of his Father in heaven. He looked at reality with the desire to see God at work, and that shaped the reality he saw.

Imagination can travel further than understanding and reason. It can connect the seen to the unseen. It recognizes the past in the present and the future travelling toward them both. My discoveries that week at Scargill, while reading Mark's Gospel, were what I needed to see and feel at that time in my journey of faith. They were discoveries that I needed to receive as God's communication. Yet if I now say, 'That's all I will find in Mark,' I shall miss the point, for, led by imagination, I can return again and discover something else. In the words of another hymn, 'the Lord has yet more light and truth to break forth from his word' (George Rawson, 1807–89).

For reflection

Read the parables in Matthew 13 and observe the imagination of Jesus at work.

Prayer suggestion

Select a biblical encounter between Jesus and another person: for example, the Samaritan woman in John 4. Read it through slowly, and then again. During the second reading, notice what catches your eye or makes you want to think further. Pause with that part of the story and begin to consider what was happening at that moment. These questions may help:

- What does this story tell you about Jesus?
- What emotions are being felt by the characters in the story?
- Where would you imagine yourself to be in this story?
- What experiences in your life does it remind you of?
- What questions does this raise for you?

Consider your response to these questions and pray them over with the Spirit of God.

For discussion

How much faith are you prepared to place in imagination as a helpful way of exploring the Bible?

'A yearning faith' link to 'A gospel place'

For many people, their faith is a very personal matter. It is about their convictions and motivation, and is based on their experience of God within the texture of their life. They might speak of knowing inner peace, which gives them a sign that God is with them. This peace can be very real and precious.

Sometimes, though, we can overlook the context in which personal faith is nurtured and grows. The context will include other people, events and the place where that faith is being developed. Do we underestimate the importance of place in the shaping of our faith and spirituality?

These days, many places have become the focus of a search for meaning and faith, including traditional sites such as Holy Island or Iona. Pilgrimages to places of prayer and spiritual renewal are very popular well beyond the Christian community, among those who are seeking spiritual depth in our shallow society. I believe it is necessary for Christian people to recognize that this is a valid part of 'seeking God'.

In the Gospels, the places where certain events happened are very important in understanding the meaning of what happened there. The exact location may no longer be known, but its influence cannot be ignored.

We need to recognize our own 'gospel places'—locations where our faith was shaped by the look and feel of the environment round about us. These places should be remembered and honoured. They helped to shape our experience of God.

A gospel place

Off the beaten track

'Can anything good come out of Nazareth?'
JOHN 1:46

It is difficult to keep Jesus on the margins of society, but it is essential that we do. Once Jesus becomes tied up with the powers that be, we begin to lose the authority of his words and life. In his lifetime he was a small-town rabbi. He skirted the cities of notoriety and influence. Instead, he used the paths and back roads of Galilee.

Jesus was born in a place that the prophets had predicted would be at the centre of divine activity: Bethlehem had its place in Jewish salvation history, but Nazareth had no such reputation. Nazareth was a poor hamlet, its name unknown beyond its own vicinity. It receives no mention in the Old Testament. The Gospel of John conveys the sense of disdain commonly felt for Nazareth, in Nathanael's response to the news that the Messiah had come from the town (John 1:46).

Nazareth was a place that just did not count. Its inhabitants revealed some of the inbred resentment and fear often found in those who are ignored and forgotten, in their own reaction to Jesus' ministry (Mark 6:1–6). They could not believe that any special blessing could come from God to such a place or to one of their own.

Where is your Nazareth? You can take that question in two ways. 'Nazareth' may describe a place, a street or a family known to you. It is too easy to believe that no good can come from such a place or group of people. 'Christ cannot be there. No work of God would be possible among them.' Are you sure? Alternatively, 'Nazareth' may describe some part of the life of your church—a group of people who are dismissed because they do not 'fit'. They are seen but not noticed. They do not count. They seem beyond the influence of God, even though they share a faith in common with the rest of the church. But are you sure?

When Jesus moved to Capernaum, he hardly moved up in the world. It was a small, untidy cluster of poorly built houses. The fishermen landed their catch on the beach. Their boats were moored to quays made from a few piled-up stones. The trade roads did not pass nearby. Tiberias, a few miles along the lakeside, could boast its Roman streets and tiled houses. Wealth poured into its streets with their well-stocked shops, and a theatre was being built, over-looking the town. This was a place that proclaimed the dominance of the Roman/Greek culture—but there is no mention in the Gospels that Jesus ever went there. He kept to the margins and spent time among those who went unnoticed.

Jesus proclaimed a kingdom, but it was a kingdom concerned with covenant more than contract. His kingdom sought that which could bring equality of opportunity. The parables of that kingdom did not use the stories and experiences of the local economy simply because they were plain to see. What Jesus saw happening among the farmers and fishermen spoke of values and beliefs that were vitally important. They represented the way his Father in heaven wished the world to be.

In this kind of local economy, when you have a large catch of fish, you ask for help from your neighbour and he responds. You land the catch together as partners, not as rivals. When your field throws up a crop of unpleasant weeds, a thoughtful neighbour wonders whether there's a rogue in the community. You sow seed over a path, despite the thin soil, because that will provide gleanings for the stranger in your midst, as commanded by your culture and law. The extraordinary generosity of a father who welcomes back a spendthrift son may be exceptional, but you recognize the hard-bitten greed of the elder son who has forgotten that the land belongs to the Lord.

The covenant kingdom that Jesus proclaimed had core values of justice, righteousness, compassion and mercy. Those values took on flesh in his ministry. Among the struggling and the overlooked, he came as hope for new life. Among the wealthy and influential, he came as an alternative to their power-driven lives. He came with his Father's promise of good news for the poor. His presence turned the most unlikely of spots into gospel places.

Can you live with this Capernaum Christ? Read Mark 1:21–28. You will not go far without the touch of his love. Without it, the demands of his lifestyle will be too much. You will need to notice that his first healing in Capernaum was one that released the entrapped. You, like the possessed man, may resist the presence of Jesus, but you will need to take on board that his expectations are absolute. He heals with a purpose. The gift of trust in him is not yours to keep hidden; it is a means of proclaiming God's work of grace and life.

Jesus lived at a time when the rule of Rome had become the norm. It was no more cruel than other empires, and it was this dead hand of the 'normal' that Jesus was wishing to challenge. He could not live a compromised life.

For reflection

Read Luke 4:16–30 and consider how, through the words of Isaiah, you could turn the place where you are into a gospel place.

Prayer suggestion

Pray for people you know who are kept on the margins of our society.

For discussion

Nazareth or Capernaum: which place best describes your experience of church at present?

A place with water

In those days Jesus came from Nazareth of Galilee and was baptized by John in the Jordan.
MARK 1:9

People still come to be baptized in the Jordan. Now they come from all over the world. In the spring of 2006, I stood among a group of them. The Spirit now descends on people in many places, and the Father's gift through the Son is no longer confined to the banks of one stretch of water. Yet a few moments beside the slow-moving waters of the biblical river can become a time of transfiguration.

Standing beside the Jordan, I tried to remember my own baptism when I was only 14, many miles away. A lot of water has flowed under the bridge since then! I have never doubted the importance of my baptism—for me it was the right time and the right place—but I recognize that I can tend to forget the meaning of baptism for my life as a Christian. As I looked at the rather muddy waters of the river, I wondered what difference it should make, if any, that this water is a place of baptism. I would have an answer shortly.

I remembered a conversation that I had had with a man, a few days before I left for Israel. He was a deeply disillusioned Baptist who felt that he had been baptized too early in his Christian experience. He, like me, had been baptized as a teenager, but we wondered together whether churches in the 1960s and '70s baptized too many people in their teens who were not ready for a lifetime's commitment to Christ. Of course, it is easy to say in reply, 'Who is ever ready?' But I have met too many puzzled and struggling Christians, baptized in that era, not to wonder whether my disillusioned friend had a point. The pressure to conform can be

37

intense. The intoxicating mixture of hormones and new faith can propel a young person into a decision that can be momentous at the time, but later may be regretted. Have you noticed how baptism, for some, seems to be a prelude to departure from the church?

The baptism of Jesus could be treated as a model. He was baptized at the beginning of his ministry—but not at the start of his life of faith. Long before he stepped into the waters of the Jordan, his nurture in his people's faith had begun in home and synagogue. There had been many years of preparation for this moment of decision and revelation. He was no longer a young man. We do not know how Jesus had spent his time in Nazareth of Galilee. We can assume that he was a local craftsman—a worker in wood who knew something about building construction—and that this would have introduced him to the economic and social life of the area. He would have travelled the district in pursuit of his trade for many years. Perhaps he already knew this stretch of the Jordan's bank well.

We were a company of Baptists and Anglicans that morning beside the Jordan. My Anglican colleague offered a renewal of baptism promises to any who wished it—and this provoked an impromptu church meeting among the Baptists! No one was against what was being offered, although some wondered about the necessity. For them, each time they received the bread and wine it was an opportunity to renew those promises. Others were glad to accept the opportunity, but the request had made us all pause and wonder what our baptism meant to us now. And so together, Baptist minister and Anglican priest, we served those who wished it. The promises were heard again, water was poured over out-stretched hands and all shared in a time of silence and prayer.

Just along the bank, all was song and laughter. There was a group of Roman Catholics from the USA. Their priest was up to his hips in the river—not like this fussy Baptist who had remained decidedly dry throughout our process! They too were sharing in a renewal of vows. As I watched, however, a young teenager came forward and, after a brief conversation and to the evident delight of the whole company, was immersed in the water. She emerged with a radiant smile, to be embraced by her friends and a singing priest.

I talked to the Catholic priest and the teenage girl as we wandered back to our coaches. I resisted the temptation to explore the technical issues of theology and practice in his Church with the priest. Once he learnt that I was a Baptist, his smile just got bigger, and he asked, 'So what do you make of that?' I ventured to ask what his bishop would make of it. 'Special place! Special time!' he replied.

The teenager introduced me to her grandmother, who was incoherently full of smiles and tears. I wondered what prayers of hers had been answered that day. The youngster smiled her faith at me, and I was disarmed by the simplicity of the moment. Of course, she could not say all that the day had meant to her. What events life will bring to her, unbidden and unwanted, cannot be anticipated, and I am left hoping that the nurture she receives in her parish will make and sustain a faith that sees the special in the ordinary. I hope she will not feel betrayed by the power of the moment, in the dimmer light of everyday life back home.

Baptism is about choosing to see life differently—discovering that there is a divine providence working, which is not at our command and is not always obvious. If this discovery is forgotten, or never embraced at all, disillusionment will set in. Baptism should be received with humility. God is very much used to taking unfinished products and working on them. It is only our arrogance that tells us we can do anything to deserve his gifts.

For reflection

Ephesians 1—3 might have been written as an explanation of what it means to become a Christian, for people being prepared for baptism. What do these chapters tell us about being baptized?

Prayer suggestion

Pray for all those making baptismal promises for themselves or others.

For discussion

What does your baptism mean to you now?

A hill with a view

Peter said to Jesus, 'Rabbi, it is good for us to be here.'
MARK 9:5

I have sometimes thought that the story of Jesus' transfiguration reads like an event that came after his resurrection rather than before it. Perhaps that is because it does have echoes of Easter experience —and why not? All the Gospels were written after the resurrection. Easter created a faith that was bound to influence the images and ideas that shaped the way in which the stories of Jesus were told.

Yet it is strange to think that Mark might have pulled a resurrection story back into the lifetime of Jesus, when he follows his account of the transfiguration with a conversation between the disciples in which they puzzle over what it means to rise from the dead (9:10). If the event had happened after he had risen, this would have been quite contradictory—though it makes sense that the transfiguration could not be spoken of until the disciples understood its meaning in the light of the resurrection (v. 9).

Whichever view you take, the resurrection was a unique event, but it also revealed something that was always the case: Jesus is the unique Son of God. And, at certain moments in his ministry, glimpses of clarity were given to the disciples about that reality. The transfiguration was an invitation to look at Jesus from a different angle. It was as if a veil was being pulled back, revealing what was always there but unseen. There are unseen elements in all our lives, which we can easily ignore amid the ordinary demands of every day.

The appearance of Moses and Elijah has been described as a kind of salvation-history summit conference. They had much in common with Jesus' disciples. Both Moses and Elijah received a deeper awareness of the presence of God on a mountain. They, like the disciples, saw what was hidden as their struggles and their faith were brought to a place where the wider picture could be seen. On his wilderness mountain-top, the discouraged Elijah received insight and courage to take on what was still in store for him (1 Kings 19:11–19). Moses toiled up the mountain of Sinai and returned from the cloud of God's presence with the Ten Commandments. He did this not once but twice, for the people of God did not respond well to the guidance that God was offering (Exodus 32—33). The way of struggle and sacrifice was a well-known path for the great prophets of Israel long before Jesus followed it to the cross.

Ever aware of the danger of misrepresentation, Jesus warned his disciples against speaking of their experience up in the heights of northern Galilee. The voice of God had spoken from the cloud. Now as never before, they would have to pay attention to him, not to their amazement and pride.

Some Christians attach great importance to location. They have a spirituality of place. For them, the physical setting of significant events is to be honoured and protected. Others would prefer to remember the experience of what happened in a place rather than the place itself. It is best not to treat this choice as an 'either–or'. It is probably as important to treasure the memory of a place of inspiration as to live still with what inspired us.

Reflect for a while on this imaginative reconstruction of Peter's thoughts about the experience.

So I thought to myself: Where's he taking us now? My fisherman's legs weren't used to climbing hills! And when we arrived... No, of course it wasn't the lack of oxygen! I saw what I saw. Jesus looked different. He glowed. It was the brightness of a new dawn. There, high in the hills with our lake lost in the haze, I saw him in a completely different light.

Well, I had to say something, didn't I? Me, keep silent? It was such a privilege! No one could take this moment away from us. This was my opportunity to get it right! The others were as tongue-tied as ever. Just as well Thomas wasn't there, or he would have given me one of his looks.

But I couldn't contain myself. The Teacher was wonderful, and his companions were amazing. This was a time to worship—a moment to capture. Why not do something symbolic? My synagogue teacher would have been proud of me. Moses and Elijah were God's travelling people. Tents—travel huts—that's what they knew. We could build them. They would become tabernacles for the presence of the Lord. As I said later, Moses and Elijah didn't say no—but the others pointed out that they didn't say yes either. I was wrong again. They didn't need what we could offer.

It made me think. If they didn't need what I offered, what did they need? Was I seeing it from the wrong angle? Does God need our special places, or does he know no limits? What awaited us as we tramped down from the mountain would begin to change our attitude to our religion and its sacred places for ever.

For reflection

Read 2 Peter 1:16–18 and consider the importance of experience over place.

Prayer suggestion

Thank God for the places where you have been aware of his majestic glory.

For discussion

Describe places that have been important for you in your journey of faith and say what they mean to you now.

Faith in a valley

Jesus replied, 'A man was going down from Jerusalem to Jericho...'
LUKE 10:30

A few years ago, I travelled in Jordan and stayed at a hotel on the shores of the Dead Sea. On my last day there, I was up early to see the sunrise. The sun would rise behind me, first lighting the hills of Judea across the water from my room's balcony.

The air was still and very cool as I gazed across the water, watching for any sign that night was ending. The first sense of the coming dawn was a subtle change in the greys, purples and blues of the landscape around me. Above, the sky mirrored the changes with just a hint of pink and ochre. Then, suddenly, like so many lights being switched on, the rising sun glinted on windows high in the far distance.

Jerusalem! More and more they came—those bright, intense reflections—and gradually I could discern the shapes of buildings on the Mount of Olives. It was a moment of discovery and delight. 'A city set on a hill cannot be hidden': it was there for all to see. My thoughts teemed with pleasure and anguish. Such beauty! Such history! Such importance! So much despair! So much frustration! So much regret! This is Jerusalem today, a place that reduced Jesus to tears and for whose peace he came.

The light of the rising sun created a shadow which descended slowly down the flanks of the hills. Eventually, with Jerusalem in bright sunlight and already disappearing into a heat haze, my gaze moved to where the sun had not yet reached. The broad valley floor was still in gloom: it had not yet been touched by direct light. And there, much nearer to me, was Jericho.

I had been lost in the wonder of the sunrise upon Jerusalem, and Jericho had had to wait her turn. I realized that it had been ever thus. Among the cities of the world, Jericho is one of the longest to be continuously occupied. From the beginning of time, her people have always had a longer wait for the dawn than those who live on the heights above. The sun rises last on the people who live in the bottom of the valley. This was a price they were ready to pay for farming in the once-rich vegetation of the fertile Jordan valley. In the light of the city's contemporary experience, it is a poignant symbol of need and circumstance.

A long, hard climb out of Jericho through a narrow valley ends at the Mount of Olives. It is a track as old as human life in that area. It rises hundreds of metres—a long climb that is not completed quickly. This path to a city on a hill, from another city which, at both dawn and dusk, lies in the shadows, is not an easy one.

Jesus made that climb from Jericho in the hours before Palm Sunday. His final encounter with the city in the valley is recorded in Mark 10, Matthew 20 and Luke 18—19. Each Gospel records the experience in a different way, but they all agree that Jesus performed a miracle of healing there. In Mark, Jesus heals Bartimaeus while entering Jericho. In Matthew, he heals two blind men on the way to that steep climb out of the city. Luke follows Mark but includes his own story of Zacchaeus, together with a parable that has critical overtones about Israel and her failure to follow the path that God had set for his people.

At the heart of the occasion is the question of Jesus, 'What is it that you want me to do for you?' The two blind men were unhesitating: they wanted their sight (Matthew 20:32–33). What a question for Jesus to ask! I cannot imagine that the Gospel writers missed its impact and irony. Within a few sentences, the reader will be deeply involved in the final days of Jesus, but that question from Jericho travels through the shadowed valley to the sunlit outskirts of Jerusalem. Just what is it that we want Jesus to do for us as he follows his God-given path to the cross?

There is an answer in the question that Jesus asked the blind men. They answer by asking to be able to see. The gift of sight would provide them with opportunity and meaning. They would be able to take a place in their society which would not be defined by people's perception of their disability. The confusion of noise that made them shout above the crowd to Jesus would be a thing of the past. Their dependence on the fickle help of other people would be over.

God waits to receive our requests and responds with grace and compassion. He then takes us to the cross and bids us watch and wonder until 'the dawn from on high... [breaks] upon us; to give light to those who sit in darkness and in the shadow of death, to guide our feet into the way of peace' (Luke 1:78–79).

For reflection

Read the three Gospel accounts of Jesus in Jericho, and ponder what we can learn from their differences.

Prayer suggestion

Pray for those who are always the last to receive from the generosity of others.

For discussion

If Jesus came to your church asking the question he asked at Jericho, what would you answer and how do you think he would respond?

A healing space

Jesus answered them, 'My Father is still working, and I also am working.'
JOHN 5:17

These were the words of Jesus to a man whom he healed at the pool near ancient Jerusalem's Sheep Gate. I once sat near the remains of this area in the Muslim quarter of the Old City in Jerusalem. Files of tourists, from all over the world, wandered among the local people. The cries of water salesmen mingled with the instructions of guides. Nearby was the Crusader-built church of St Anne's. Its clean lines and open design contrasted strongly with the perplexing intricacies of the Orthodox churches we had visited. I sat by the wall to watch.

People emerged from the church in different ways. Many had blank expressions: another hour; more old stones! Some left talking animatedly. It almost seemed as if they were oblivious to where they had been. 'Is the camera still working? ... When's the next coffee break? ... If that woman in our group doesn't stop asking her fool-questions, we won't see half of what we've come here to see! ... Do you think people still worship God here?'

Now there's a question! It is one that John's Gospel considers in various ways, for at its heart is this debate: Was Jesus who he claimed to be? Could he have had a special relationship with God the Father which had priority over all others? Could someone who seemed to have so little time for the sabbath have been doing God's work?

The pool of Bethzatha lay outside the walls of Jerusalem. It had started as a reservoir (2 Kings 18:17), but by the time of Jesus it had become a place where many ill people gathered, believing that there was a healing presence in the waters. It is usual these days to treat John 5:4 as a later addition, but it captures some of the superstitious background to the place and the whole issue of healing in the time of Jesus. Healing was a matter of chance—being in the right place at the right time. The waters were a place of waiting. No one was too sure when the healing moment would arrive, and some of the people whom Jesus saw that day had waited a long time. The provider of healing did not appear to be in a hurry to make things better for them.

The unwell knew their place: it was outside the city walls. They were only a few metres from the magnificent temple that Herod was having built, but they could not go there. Jesus knew his place too: he moved among them. His presence brought the temple to them. His work with the Father was in the flesh-and-blood encounters of his daily life, and at the centre of those encounters was healing.

This story has made me reconsider the relationship of healing to proclamation in the ministry of Jesus. I remember when the Baptist Union Health and Healing Group first started in the life of our denomination, back in the 1970s. There were mixed reactions. For many people, it was a restored ministry. For others, there were seemingly insurmountable questions and problems, many of which seemed to be fed by fear. I cannot avoid the feeling that, both in my ministry and in the life of many churches (not just Baptist), the healing ministry is—like the positioning of the pool of Bethzatha—'outside our city walls'.

I am well aware of all the issues! Like much today, the healing ministry seems to bring with it a raft of questions: 'What...?' 'How...?' and 'Why not...?' In the same way, what Jesus said and did that day at the pool provoked much debate and concern. But that is not a reason for avoiding encounters with people in real need. Instead, we should meet those needs with the grace and comfort of God the Father.

Jesus speaks of the 'working' God more than once in the Gospels. This suggests to me a God who is continually at work to restore and transform his creation, who draws in any and all who align themselves with his desire. The purpose of that restoration is to bring in 'life in all its fullness' (John 10:10, GNB), which is a matter of health and wholeness.

At the pool of Bethzatha, Jesus met a man who was alone with his problems. He, with others, was on the edge of the community, at the strange mercy of a god who might or might not turn up. This situation had gone on for years, and Jesus rightly wondered whether the man still wished to get better. Long-term ill health can be a destroyer of all hope and motivation.

'How much longer do we have to pray for this, John?' That was a heartfelt question from a member of our congregation recently. The situation he was talking about has been a matter of prayer for many of us for a long time, but it is teaching us a very important lesson. While we might think we know everything that might be the answer to our prayers, perhaps we have to ask to *see* the answer rather than assuming we know it. Intercession is about joining God in his work of restoration and transformation, not simply sending messages of encouragement and support.

For reflection

Compare this story with Mark 2:1–12, looking for similarities and differences and what they reveal about the healing ministry of Jesus.

Prayer suggestion

Start a prayer list of people for whom you will pray regularly.

For discussion

Do you agree that the ministry of healing is neglected in our churches today?

A hill outside a city wall

'Truly this man was God's Son!'
MARK 15:39

They were his words, not ours. We were not allowed to get that close. I was grateful for them, and yet also puzzled. Are we not all sons of God? Is this not our calling as the people of Israel?

Surely he couldn't know our scriptures that well? We always called our king a son of God, as a sign of honour and obedience. Was this officer one of the renegade Jews that had taken the Emperor's coin? Whatever he meant, he spoke for himself, not us.

Our feet were sore and our souls were empty. This was a death like no other. Jesus had given so much, but there was still so much to give. The men had warned against coming to Jerusalem. We hadn't been consulted: Jesus included us far more than we were included at home but when it came to decisions, we were just the support crew.

So we watched. It had to be at a distance. The men were long gone—they knew they would be the next targets. But you would have thought that one of them would have stayed within range. Jesus' death was the last act of a lovely life, and its terror was awful. The pain throbbed through his body. To see it was to share the suffering. Why couldn't the others have stayed?

He had spoken with them so often. Surely they understood more than they said they did? They said it was as if, in the last days, he had been overwhelmed by a desire to explain—consumed with the desire that they should know what it all meant. But it was so different. His stories had dried up, and when he did tell one, it was so political that even our Galilean hotheads felt uncomfortable.

He seemed to be challenging everything: the temple would fall; Jerusalem would be sacked; the Passover meal was all about him. It was too much. Was he out of his mind? Had it all come to this—a broken Messiah, disappointed and disappointing his people?

There was no need to stay long. At least the Roman authorities respected our traditions. The body is in its tomb. Some of us will get up early and do what is required to that body. It's the last thing we can do.

Some women were there...
MARK 15:40 (GNB)

I noticed them. I thought they would have come closer: we wouldn't have stopped them. Some of them looked pretty. These travelling preachers always attract a few. Lonely wives, sad spinsters, you know the type—no man in their life, so why not let fancy fly with a golden-tongued rabbi?

Apparently he was quite a star in Galilee. I travelled through there once. They're a strange lot—all business and hooded looks. You never really knew where you were with them. Mind you, anyone in our uniform must have made them shudder. By God, there had been some crucifixions in Galilee. It was the only way to put them down.

He must have been a young lad when all that happened. I wonder whether he thought he would ever end up on a cross. He probably did. Rome has killed so many of them that way. But why come all the way to Jerusalem to get himself executed? If he was going to stir up trouble, why not do it nearer home? At least that way his family could take care of his body after we'd finished with it.

I couldn't tell whether the women were his family. As I say, they wouldn't come close enough. But what were they to me? It was the man on the cross who compelled me to speak like I did. I surprised myself. I've seen my fill of cross-deaths. You don't look any more.

I was just doing my job: strip down; hands; feet; slash and stab and then up they go and pray for a short dying. And in his case, that's what happened. He didn't hang around for long—excuse my little joke.

You can speculate on why I said it for as long as you like. It was as if the words were given to me. They were sort of pulled out of me, spoken before I knew what I was saying. And don't ask me why I said them. Ask the person who told you I did. What I'd like to know is why he's still talking about Jesus, now he's dead and gone.

For reflection

This imaginative exploration of the death of Jesus is based solely on the account in Mark 15:21–41. Compare it with other Gospel accounts of the same event, especially John 19:16–30.

Prayer suggestion

Read one of the Gospel accounts and pray for the people it reminds you of in your own life who need the challenge and comfort of God.

For discussion

How close would you have been to the cross if you had been there?

A view from a hill

Every day he was teaching in the temple, and at night he would go out and spend the night on the Mount of Olives.
LUKE 21:37

Now it's all over, I've come to sit here and remember. We used to come here with him. All that talk in the temple used to exhaust him and us! It wasn't physically tiring, more a case of nervous exhaustion. You never knew what was going to happen next.

This place has seen so much. It's seen me in tears. It's seen me hardly able to contain myself with excitement. We had hopes for so much, and it looked as if our Master was going to fulfil them all.

I don't think Jesus ever did anything that he didn't plan to happen. Actually, there is one exception, and I'll speak of that later —but it was obvious that our nights spent on the slopes of the Mount of Olives were quite deliberate. Sometimes I think he could not get out of the scriptures. He constantly seemed to be reworking them into what he did and said.

I could see what he was trying to do, though. He had to convince our people that he himself was the visitation of God that the old-time prophets had prepared them for. And what better place to do it than on the Mount of Olives? Its tree-strewn slopes and numerous wine presses and tombs made it impressive enough. The view it gave of the temple as the building reached its completion was stunning. You can stand at its top and see the wilderness and the Jordan valley in one direction; then you turn, and there is the shining glory of the Temple Mount. You can look in every direction and see reminders of God's story in a landscape of hills, trees and wilderness.

More than that, Herod is making so much of the city now. You can see the stadium from here, and the theatre. You won't get me to either of them, but they will truly be one of the wonders of the world. The Romans expect you to dance to their tune, but they reward faithful allies, and Herod and his family are certainly those!

Jesus always saw more than meets the eye, and he was right: the seeds of destruction are there too. We never learn—alliances with foreign powers never work in our favour. Our history is littered with the broken promises of our rulers and their erstwhile allies. There is no one we can trust but the Lord.

Perhaps it was just too much for our religious leaders to take in: a man from Galilee standing on the Mount of Olives, claiming that the temple was not a lasting sign of God's favour. After all, don't we believe that God has made his dwelling place on Zion, and that he will be there in the Holy of Holies? I don't think they could entertain the possibility of God appearing on any other hillside. As far as they were concerned, God knows his place and should keep to it!

I think their opposition broke Jesus' heart. This hillside witnessed his tears as well as mine. Peter told me that he was in a terrible state a couple of nights ago. Peter said he could only guess at what had gone on, but the Master had the look of someone who had experienced despair right to his very core. It was as if he was prepared to walk away from us all and God, Peter thought.

I was not witness to that, but I did see him cry. That was the unplanned moment I was talking about, something that he could not have anticipated. We'd just climbed up from Bethany and were taking in the view—for some of us it was the first time—and then we noticed Jesus with tears streaming down his face. He couldn't have planned that. It was obvious he could not contain himself. Jerusalem has been no friend of prophets down the years, but this prophet was going to give them another chance. And they took it.

Or rather, they took him. We couldn't stop them. The women said we'd been lulled to sleep by the smell of the new wine being made at the garden called Gethsemane. But it wasn't that wine I was bothered with. It was what Jesus had said about the food and drink of the Passover meal—about them being his body and his blood. I'd never heard him speak words like those before. He sort of slipped them in before we realized what was happening. The Passover routine is familiar enough. It's not something you tamper with, but Jesus never let a little bit of tradition get in the way of what he called his 'new wine'. I will certainly remember those words for a long time, but I'm still not sure what they mean. I'll have to ask the others, if I ever find them.

Perhaps we should have stayed among the olive trees. It would have been so easy to slip away under cover of darkness. But Jesus just seemed to wait there. It was as if he had nothing more to say to them, to us—to God, even. As we say, a willing spirit is stronger than the weakness of our flesh. A cloak of silence seemed to descend on him. Some of us tried to make a fight of it when the guards came, but you could never really be violent when Jesus was around.

Anyway, he's dead and buried now, and I'm meeting a friend. We're going to travel as far as Emmaus. It's safer there. I've so much to talk about. I'm not sure whether I feel let down or just left behind. I'm not sure what life without the Master will be like now.

For reflection

Read Luke 19:28–44; Mark 14:12–25, 32–36, 43–50; Luke 24:13–17.

Prayer suggestion

Pray for someone known to you who is realizing that they are unsure about Jesus and is wondering what to do about it.

For discussion

Where are the places you go to, that help you think over what you are experiencing in your life at the moment?

Paddington station in Advent

I will give you as a light to the nations,
that my salvation may reach to the end of the earth.
ISAIAH 49:6

Isaiah speaks often of God's Servant, and it is thought that he is talking about the nation of Israel. Israel was the creation of God—a people called into existence to be a sign of God among the nations of the earth. At the time when Isaiah was speaking of God's servant, however, Israel did not exist as a country. Its tribes were in exile among the communities of Assyria and Babylon. So it might be more accurate to say that his vision of God's servant was not a description of Israel as a historical state among other states, but rather a description of how to be a community. God's servant, according to Isaiah, is a way of being humans together, underpinned by the intention of God to draw all people to himself (Isaiah 51:4). Israel has the look of a people who are shaped by the atoning love of God.

During Advent especially, Christians see this vision of Isaiah reflected in Jesus and the community of disciples he created (1 Peter 2:9–10). It is a community that began within the region of Israel but quickly took on the accents and lifestyles of many cultures. The disciples of Jesus are not simply to be a light to the nations: they *are* the nations! So Advent is a time to celebrate the international flavour of the community of faith that the gospel has created through Christ and his followers.

And so we come to Paddington station, where I find myself one afternoon in December, waiting to be taken home to Bath. As I stand near the baguette bar and drag my eyes away from the information boards that assure me my train is on time, I notice that I am in the middle of an intricate community of people. Some, like me, wait in the queue for a drink. The contact with the assistant is brief and our eyes hardly meet, let alone our hands. But I turn, and there in front of me I witness a joyous reunion. I had noticed him pacing the concourse, anxiously checking that the platform had not been changed. Now she has arrived and they are embedded in an embrace of desire and fun that is oblivious to the rushing 'suits' who have worked their way up from Wales, tapping on their laptops.

For the commuters, the station is no more than a place of transit. But for Maisie and George it means far more than that. They were watching the embracing couple, too, and went on to introduce themselves to me. They told me their names because, they said, I didn't seem to be rushing somewhere—unlike most other people. (I was waiting hopefully for my train to be announced as actually running!) So they tell me that they have grandchildren in Exeter and they are about to embark on their pre-Christmas visit. I find out a lot about their cat and the neighbours and their pride in their daughter and the fact that they have been forced to stop using the car (and the last time they used Paddington, there were steam trains!).

So it goes on—people chatting, rushing, standing, pacing, looking for information, waiting... oh, so many of us waiting. And in each of us there is a story, a 'day in the life of', paths crossing in a glorious temple to our insatiable desire to travel and arrive.

This is how Paddington station becomes an Advent place. There is something about its check-ins, shopping mall provision, grey-suited commuters, blaring announcements, frantic turnaround of trains and people that makes it impersonal and threatening, but that is not all that is going on. It is also a place of communion, sometimes brief and transient, at other times deep and full of longing—and did I spot a young pregnant woman on a donkey led by a man with dreamy eyes? No, of course not! But because of *their* journey, nowhere is off limits to the Advent presence of God.

For reflection

Read Isaiah 43:1–13.

Prayer suggestion

Go to a place where people are leaving and arriving, to watch and pray!

For discussion

What everyday places—like a railway station—can become places that make you think about the presence of God?

Empty streets

By the tender mercy of our God,
the dawn from on high will break upon us,
to give light to those who sit in darkness
and in the shadow of death,
to guide our feet into the way of peace.
LUKE 1:78–79

It was late at night as I made my way back from the theatre to the station. My head was still thudding with the beat of the music and my heart racing from the spectacle of *Jesus Christ Superstar*. This was its first outing in the 1960s, when it all seemed very daring and alternative.

As I stood waiting to cross the road, a young boy wandered out of the shadows and stood waiting with me. The traffic paused and we crossed the road together. I hadn't realized he had spoken to me until he repeated his request: 'I said, got some cash for a drink?' He was obviously nervous and I wasn't sure how to respond. I felt that it was an intrusion and wondered whether I was being set up. I looked around but there was no one about and, as we reached the station entrance, he suddenly picked up a discarded food bag. He scrabbled in it and pulled out half a sandwich, which he began to eat. I bought his drink, but it gave me no pleasure because I knew in my heart of hearts that he was calling me into a world I could not cope with.

Another night, another city, and I dodged the late-night traffic to make a long-distance call at the street booth. By the time I was finished, the cars, buses, bikes and trams of Kolkata, India, no longer thronged the road outside my hostel. In their place were tiny little fires, with small figures standing round them or huddling down on the tarmac to sleep. Many were children and, as I passed, they looked up and called after me. I stood by the gate, struggling to stay and watch. I felt like the intruder this time.

One lad got up and tugged my arm to lead me toward their fire. I moved a little way but not too far. It is so easy to let wariness be our guide when in the unknown. He smiled and watched for my hand to offer him something. By signs and mime, I indicated that I needed to go to my bed. The whirring fan in my room didn't seem such a nuisance that night.

I was up early the next morning. I had decided I needed to do something. I went out into the street, but there was no sign of the youngsters. The blackened coals of their fire, like the many others, were now being scattered by the chaotic weaving of the early morning traffic. I had received an invitation the night before, which caution and fear had prevented me from accepting—and the chance did not come again, for that day I flew home.

Home was once a Buckinghamshire village with a single street, along which were arranged shops, pubs, homes and my church building. Early one Christmas Day afternoon, I walked the street. I was alone and the wind was stirring the tinsel on the outdoor Christmas trees. As I walked, I could hear the noise of people celebrating in the flats above the shops. Bursts of laughter mingled with music and the sound of party games. Occasionally there was a raucous version of a carol, mixed with Slade's 'Merry Christmas'. But it was second-hand joy. I could hear it but did not feel part of it. The chilling isolation created by the 'family' Christmas enveloped me. It only takes the thickness of a brick wall to create a gap that cannot be bridged.

I am glad to have had the chance, a few years ago, to walk the streets of the Old City of Jerusalem when the traders had closed down and the crowds had gone. It was a precious walk, as there is usually so little time to think in that place. The demands of the pilgrim way, the incessant calls to see and buy, the need to be engaged with the history, politics and theology of the place, give you no peace. So I took the chance to be alone and try to let something take root in my searching and faith, from that city which offers so much to disturb and challenge us. And the moment was given, under the arch of the Damascus Gate, in the shape of a young mother and child. He backed away from me so she held out her hand and he gratefully clung to it. Firmly held, he smiled at me, because her motherly act made the empty street and a stranger less threatening.

Empty streets can contain encounters that disturb.

For reflection

Read Luke 14:12–24.

Prayer suggestion

Consider the encounters that you have experienced in any one day's walk through the streets, and seek the presence of God in them.

For discussion

Do you have any stories of similar encounters to mine? What effect have they had on you?

'A gospel place' link to 'Gospel encounters'

Gospel places may be a hillside overlooking Jerusalem or Paddington Station at rush hour. They are locations that open our eyes to God and what we believe. They may contain the memory of events that occurred there, like the river bank of Jordan or the streets of Kolkata.

They reveal more than can be taken in by the naked eye. They are invitations to seek the presence of God anywhere and everywhere.

Where can I go from your spirit?
Or where can I flee from your presence? ...
If I take the wings of the morning
and settle at the farthest limits of the sea,
even there your hand shall lead me,
and your right hand shall hold me fast,
PSALM 139:7, 9–10

The 'spirituality of place' has become increasingly important to me. I think it had always been there, but the Christian tradition in which I was brought up did not really encourage it.

Now I know that there are places I have visited in my life, as well as places that I regularly see, that carry for me a feeling of the presence of God. I find it hard to describe—they are, as it were, the sacrament of what my senses reveal to me. In them there are also gospel encounters. In the next sequence of reflections, I describe a number of encounters in the life of Jesus where we can see the gospel at work.

Gospel encounters

Author! Author!

I wrote about all that Jesus did and taught.
ACTS 1:1

The Gospels emerge from the Easter faith of the first Christian communities. In the light of the resurrection, they are words of praise and thanksgiving to the Creator of us all, who has shared his rescuing love with us in Jesus. In the words of Peter, Jesus was 'a man attested to you by God with deeds of power, wonders, and signs... handed over to you according to the definite plan... of God... raised up... having received from the Father the promise of the Holy Spirit' (Acts 2:22–23, 33).

The Gospels were written and compiled by people who were thrilled by the coming of Jesus. They wanted their hearers and readers to have the sort of gospel encounter that they described— encounters with the Spirit of Jesus that would disturb, encourage, comfort and transform them.

In some liturgical traditions, the congregation is expected to stand for the reading from one of the Gospels. It is a wonderful moment in the service, a moment when we hear again the definitive action of God the Father, Son and Holy Spirit. It is to be received with praise and expectant prayer, rather than being a time to settle back and think, 'I've heard this bit before...'

How casual we can become! We surround ourselves with umpteen Bible translations and animated DVDs of the life of Jesus, we pore over daily Bible reading notes and act out scenes from his life, perhaps with added humour to help us hear the meaning. Yet often the energy of his story is absent. We may no longer sing the words 'Tell me the old, old story' but I fear that is how we think of the gospel—not exactly past its sell-by date, but maybe not the good news it once was.

The Gospel writers would not have understood this attitude. Mark cannot wait to make plain what he is talking about. Without qualification and with total candour he announces what he is writing. Before introducing us to the words of Isaiah proclaiming the future, he declares, 'The beginning of the good news of Jesus Christ, the Son of God' (1:1). He doesn't beat about the bush; he concedes nothing to people who would argue. He knows what he believes about Jesus and states it clearly. He is not writing a story, although it may read like one. He is not writing biography, although he includes biographical material about Jesus. He is writing a committed, faith-driven, God-praising message of good news.

Luke (1:1–4) is more measured. He sounds more urbane. Here is a thinker's Gospel. He knows his material and has done his research. This is not going to be an election broadcast on behalf of the East Mediterranean Christian Alliance Party. Luke does not work with soundbites or instant-access images. He is writing for people who want to sense the human in the divine drama worked out in Jesus. He populates his telling with unforgettable characters, such as the good Samaritan, the forgiving father and his two sons, Zacchaeus and Simeon. He wants to show his God-seeking readership that the young Christian faith is deeply serious about its founder and his movement of the Holy Spirit.

Matthew stays hidden in his writing. He makes no assertive declaration, like that of Mark. He does not spell out his method or motivation, as Luke does, although he is equally convinced of the need to spell out in a logical and ordered way the reason for the emergence of the Christian way in the faith of Israel. His choice is to address, very directly, the issues around Jesus's Messiahship for a Jewish reader. As his community is struggling with increased polar-ization between synagogue and church, he dwells on the teaching of Jesus the rabbi.

John is the most explicit about his intentions in writing his

Gospel, although he waits until the last few paragraphs. Then he lets his readers know that he has been very careful in his selection (20:30–31). He has certain purposes in mind:

- He wants his readers to give themselves heart and mind to Jesus as the Christ and Son of God.
- He wants them to know that he has come to his belief after a time of searching and questioning.
- He wants them to test their discovery of Jesus by the quality of life that they now live.

The Gospel writers call us to an important task: the clear, committed communication of who Jesus was and what he means for us, in the debates and needs of today.

Every church needs a Mark, Luke, Matthew and John attitude to what it is seeking to communicate. This means that in every church there will be a continuing telling of Jesus' story with delight and passion. There will also be a careful exploration of the meaning of what he said and did, along with a desire for encounters with Jesus that engage the heart, mind and personality. There will be a desire to apply what we know of Jesus to the way we live the Christian life now. Just as we believe that the Holy Spirit was at work in the compilation of the Gospels, so the Church today needs to recognize that it is being guided by the same Spirit in its love and witness for Christ. When that happens, our behaviour will be so full of energy that no one could doubt that Jesus really is who we proclaim him to be.

For reflection

Read one of the Gospels over a period of time and notice the moments when you are made to pause and think. Receive these moments as an invitation to meet Jesus.

Prayer suggestion

Pray for those who preach in your church, that they may help all their listeners to have a gospel encounter.

For discussion

What does it mean for you to have a gospel encounter?

A conversation that changed a life

A Samaritan woman came to draw water.
JOHN 4:7

She waited. It was easier. It meant she could avoid their sideways looks and murmured comments when she came into view. The morning dragged, but she really couldn't face them. They knew her life story. God knows it had been told often enough—and, knowing some of them, she was certain the tale had grown in the telling. So she waited, and then began taking the back lanes to the edge of the town. She knew the ways that would allow her to avoid people.

Just before she emerged out of cover, she paused to see if all was clear. She was surprised by what she saw: a group of men standing around the well. She didn't recognize them from that distance. They looked out of place and they were pacing around as they talked.

She waited. Eventually the men sorted themselves out and began to walk into the town. A few minutes more and she would be done. As they disappeared from view, she made her way to the well. So preoccupied was she as she busied herself, unslinging the jar from around her back, that she almost tripped over the man as he crouched in the meagre shade of the well wall, trying to get away from the midday sun.

She took a step back. He looked exhausted. She said nothing. She saw now what had not been apparent from a distance. If he was one of the group who had gone into the town, then they were outsiders, Jews travelling to Galilee. And if they were in Samaria, they were in trouble.

He knew he wouldn't be popular, suggesting that they travel through Samaria. He didn't doubt their attachment to him but when it came to tradition they were so—well, traditional. But he gave them no choice.

It was not the time for confrontation with the Pharisees or any of the authorities. He knew they were asking about him, but now was not the time. He had got caught up in all the euphoria created by John. People thought John had lined him up as the next gift of God to the nation. He was not ready. It was happening too fast. He would choose the time and place.

So he walked his followers to Sychar. The journey was not long but he could feel the tiredness coming up from within him. It was like a deep, impenetrable thirst. It was more than physical. He knew it was coming from deep within his spirit.

The others didn't comment. They grumbled about Samaritans and their unpleasant distortions of the one true faith, but it didn't stop them from going into the town to get food. They seemed glad to get away from him for a while.

She surprised him as she nearly tripped over his feet. But she had what he wanted—a water jar. Would she do what he asked?

His question was obvious enough, but she knew only a desperate man would ask it. His Jewish accent confirmed what she suspected: he was not just a stranger but a borderliner. He didn't come from Judea—the voice sounded more Galilean. He was obviously one of those rootless Jews who could find no place to settle. They were trouble and caused trouble.

She could see his plight, but knew it was more than thirst that made him speak to her. What was he really after? Why didn't he leave her alone? Why hadn't he gone into the town with the others? Was he hiding? Or didn't he want to be noticed? What had he done to end up among people of her background? What would happen if she let him drink from her people's well? She decided to get away as quickly as possible.

He understood her anxiety. He looked in a state and he knew they were breaking every taboo in the book. All he wanted was a drink, but he feared it would develop into something more.

It did! He could not help himself. She sounded defensive. Once she pressed the culture button, he had to respond. He had been told all about the Jews and the Samaritans since childhood. 'Don't go to their villages!' 'They are heretics.' 'They may look like us but that's where the similarity ends.' 'They have taken our holy scriptures and created a God for themselves; they've even moved the holy mountain.'

He did not know where the energy came from but he just had to say it. She just had to see that withholding a cup of water just because of what had happened in the past was no way of living today.

What if they were seen? What if people misunderstood his motives? Would it matter if his disciples came back while he was still talking to her, if they rolled their eyes and shuffled their feet in the dust? He couldn't help himself. It was like a deep, surging rush of life rising up within him. This was what his life was to be: truth; trust; transformation. It was meat and drink to him.

All she had wanted to do was to get some water from the town well, but she was getting more than she had ever imagined.

All he wanted was some respite, and he found himself in a conversation that provoked more controversy.

For reflection

Read the whole story of Jesus and the woman at the well (John 4:1–42) and notice how John uses it to explain who Jesus was.

Prayer suggestion

Thank God for times when the gospel has acted as a gift of reconciliation, and pray for situations where reconciliation and understanding are still needed.

For discussion

How does this interpretation of the account in John 4 explore the brief encounter between Jesus and the woman at the well?

Renewed hope

Sitting there, clothed and in his right mind.
MARK 5:15

He watched the healer leave. He would hear of this amazing man again, but this would be their only meeting together.

The healer did not look back once as his small boat cut into the choppy surface of the lake. He had given his instructions and now the man was on his own, alone with his memories and story. But what a story!

The afternoon wind grew stronger and he pulled his clothes tighter around him. That was something new. He had been naked among the tombs and never felt the cold. Now he was well, he certainly felt it. He absent-mindedly rubbed his wrists, where the chains had chafed deep uneven grooves, now showing blue against his bony wrists. Perhaps he had better try to put on some weight! But that would not be so easy…

He had fed himself with the pigswill before. The keepers had kept their distance. They used to call him all sorts of names, laughing when he buried his face in the foul slop, pushing the pigs aside. Then their language coarsened. Pig-lover! God-hater! Satan-slave!

He was never sure what possessed him, but he'd decided to get his own back. If they were going to despise him, he would give them even more reason. What better way than to forget his own name and adopt one they all hated and feared? Legion! Hadn't the legions come and destroyed their lives? So would he! Hadn't the soldiers of Rome reduced them to being peasants serving Herod's treacherous family? He would remind them each day that they were occupied people. His shrieks would be the screams of their own captivity.

As the locals came out from the village each day, he would wipe the sleep from their eyes. He would leap on to the path and remind them that they were not in God's land but in the devil's world. So eventually the people had travelled by different paths, leaving him on his own. No one spoke to him; no one used his name. He didn't use it himself. Then, at last, he'd felt he had some company—a legion of them, but they were no friends. They beat their incessant march in his head. He was an alien in his own country.

But now, he just felt in his right mind. He could not remember how long it had been since he had felt so alert, so responsive to what was around him. He was less self-absorbed; he no longer needed to take control of what he could not control. He felt emptied and yet filled at the same time. It was as if a greater power had swept through his life and blown away all the rubbish and hurt. For the first time in ages, he could sit still and not feel the frenzy come upon him—the frenzy of escape, the frenzy of fear. He no longer needed to play at being Rome's man.

Yes! That was how he would describe it. A greater power than Rome was walking in their land. But it was a gentle power, one that did not claim a right of occupation but wanted a relationship of—what could he dare say? Compassion?

Was that why the local people had run from him now? Rome they could live with. Empires come and go, and the poor wait for a change, but this new power could turn the world upside down.

The boat was out of sight, lost in the heaving waves glinting in the sunlight. How he had longed to get into that boat! It was almost as if he was back among the tombs again, pleading for things to go his way. But it was not to be. The other side of the lake was no place for him. At least on this side of the water it could be home again.

Now he would discover who his friends really were. They used to say that about people who mourn: it is not until you confront other people with their mortality that you discover the comfort of your true companions. He knew that this was what would happen now. He had not lost his life, but something in him had died. It was as if a disease had been eating away at him from the inside out. Now it was no longer there. He was free! He was well! He was... alone again!

He realized now how disconcerting he must seem to other people. Before, the situation had been clear, settled. They knew what he was and nothing changed much. Now everything had changed. He was not in mourning for what had gone—but, in a strange way, they might be.

He had no choice. He would live as a daily example of the mercy of God, a mercy that clothes the naked and calms the troubled. He wouldn't look back. The boat was gone. His healer had told him what to do.

He started walking. He would not stop until someone listened to his story.

For reflection

Read the whole story in Mark 5:1–20 and consider why this healing caused the local population to be frightened.

Prayer suggestion

Thank God for those who work in mental health care, and pray for those who need that care while living in local communities.

For discussion

Do you agree with the view of the meditation that the man's 'unclean spirit' was a symptom of a disordered society under armed occupation?

A son's gift to his father

When the spirit saw [Jesus], immediately it threw the boy into convulsions.

MARK 9:20

He never knew it was happening until it was over. Then he could see it in the faces of the people gathered round. Sometimes he did not need to look at them to know: the pain told him. Sometimes it was a burnt arm or scorched leg; sometimes he was wet through. And there was always the fear, pounding in his heart. He could feel it throbbing through his body. It was there in the eyes of his family too. Sometimes they could hardly look at him.

They had given up trying to ask him what he felt. He had no words to describe it. All he knew was that he was not just an embarrassment, he was also a judgment. He was a curse of the Evil One on his mother and father. They even said he had been unleashed on them by the will of God for something that had happened before his birth. He could not say; he was given no voice. He was dumb before their condemnation, bruised by their rejection.

The neighbours said he should not be kept in the village. They believed he was a creature of death and so should live among the dead. He was a shadow of what he should be, so he should live among those whose spirits wandered in Sheol. Others said he should be taken to the edge of the wilderness and wait to be taken by the spirits there.

His father was his hope in life. He knew that his father's fear was not greater than his love. No matter what happened, his father protected him, arguing back when the elders came with their prayers and their hard-faced 'compassion'. His father carried him when he was too weak to walk, and kept him away from the gawping crowds.

But one day, that protection didn't seem to be working: he had never been among so many people. Yet, for once, he was not the centre of attention. His father was!

His father was pleading with the disciples of the Galilean healer, begging them to touch his boy and make him well. Those disciples looked like a flock that had lost its shepherd. They avoided his father's stare and tried to move away. But the father was not so easily put off. He began to remind them what Jesus could do. He accused them of having no faith, and even told them they were more unbelieving than himself.

The disciples were clearly upset, but his father had support from some local religious leaders, who joined in as he pursued the disciples through a growing crowd. These leaders had obviously been waiting for an opportunity to tell the disciples what they thought about Jesus. How could they believe in someone who had kept them ignorant of how to cast out evil spirits? Why had they not been able to discover his power and how to use it? How could they be sure he was so important when he kept God's gift for his own exclusive use?

At that moment, the crowd surged in a new direction and the boy was left behind, struggling to stand. Then he heard the voice of his father. That voice had never sounded so wretched, so drained of hope. Yet he was talking with Jesus himself.

His father told him later that it had been like a moment of prayer. A prayer he had never uttered before. A prayer that was torn from him by the faith of Jesus in him. A prayer that surged from his soul, that he flung in the face of Jesus. A prayer whose words he would never forget—and he prayed he would never have to utter it again. It was a prayer that expected everything of God and had so little to offer God.

Since then, many people had asked the boy what happened next. He would always say the same thing: 'It was like every other time. I did not know anything had happened until I looked at the faces of the people around me.' The ones who were present at the scene spoke of his thrashing legs and foaming mouth, but he did not know a thing until it was over.

All he knew then was that he was standing. He was at peace. Jesus was holding his hand, as if waiting to see what would happen next—like a father helping his son to walk for the first time. Jesus held his hand just long enough to make him realize he could keep his balance, then let go and walked away, gathering his disciples to him as he went.

The boy was left unscathed by his experience. The reaction of the people around him told him that he was well—and he noticed their silence.

For reflection

Read Mark 9:14–29, considering the conversation between Jesus and his disciples that followed this healing and its implications for your own prayer life.

Prayer suggestion

Use the words 'I believe; help my unbelief' as your own.

For discussion

To what extent is healing helped by what the sick person sees in the faces of those around him or her?

Faith from the dust

Throwing off his cloak, he sprang up and came to Jesus.
MARK 10:50

It was dawn over Jericho but the sun would not be warming the roadside for another couple of hours, so he pulled his cloak around him and waited for the first rays to touch his face. His sightless eyes scanned the cliffs above him. He had known every feature once, but that was long ago.

The cold morning air was tightening his skin. The familiar feel of the cloak rubbed his face as he pulled it tighter. Was it a cloak or a shroud, he used to wonder. The irony was not lost on him. Blind beggars left no inheritance: he would be tossed on to the town rubbish heap in the end, and, if no one wanted it then, his cloak would become his grave-clothes.

He couldn't remember where this one had come from. He had lost count of the number of times he had been attacked and his cloak stolen. Sometimes he would struggle and frantically tug back as the invisible thief tried to take it from him. But it wasn't really worth the effort. He could always find another among the town's rubbish.

He had had a really good cloak once, given to him by someone who had not told him their name. It had been thrust into his hands with a hasty whisper, followed by the sound of swiftly running feet.

His present cloak wasn't such good quality, but it would do. It was large. He wrapped it in such a way that he could imagine he was inside a tent and couldn't be seen. It was a place where he felt secure. Unseeing and unseen, he could hide there—as if it were a cloak of invisibility. What was the old riddle? 'Why do beggars yell?

Because they are the only living thing that turns people blind the moment they come into view. They have shout to make themselves heard.'

He didn't always shout, though. He did not want to draw attention to himself. People who had known him in the past could be cruel. Sometimes even their attempts at kindness would put him on edge. He didn't want their soft-voiced sympathy. They did not know that he had learnt to hear what people were *really* saying by the tone of their voice. He could read the sound as well as he could once have studied their faces.

But it was the passing strangers he feared most. For them, he was cloaked in suspicion. They did not know his story. To them, he was just one more dust-covered social reject. They could not know— neither did they try to discover—why he was like he was. Was it something he had done? Was it his parents' fault? Was his blindness a punishment? Or was he a fake?

The religious could be even more vile. Their devotion to purity made the whole world unclean. They were glad he hid in his cloak: it kept him apart from them. They could skirt his dirty sinfulness without fear of contamination. He was God's warning—this was his purpose. He was the visible threat of an invisible God who had no compassion except for the righteous. He was unrighteousness in the flesh! He was something to step over and avoid, a God-given sign of disobedience for a people who had forgotten to be holy.

Well, he was fed up with being someone's sermon illustration. He wanted a life. He wanted healing. He wanted to know that his life had not been in vain, that he could be more than shrouded breath with the occasional scrap of kindness flung in his direction. He wanted to breathe in life in all its fullness. He had not been born to start the day in despair. He didn't want to wait for the sun's rays to warm him long after the dawn, like the rest of Jericho. He didn't want to be known as the son of Timaeus who could always be found begging from the pilgrims making their way up the track to Jerusalem.

Suddenly he felt the first surge of warmth from the sun as it crested the ridge far above him, and with it came the murmur of an approaching crowd. It was time for work! Pilgrims were easy pickings, good for a quick guilt-offering before the priests took their share.

Then he heard a name that he had never thought to hear mentioned in his presence—a name that could give him the future he longed for. He was on his feet, shouting as he had never done before, his cloak left behind like an empty shroud.

For reflection

The sources for this meditation are Mark 10:46–52; Luke 19:1–10; Isaiah 53; and conversations with people who live on the streets of Bath.

Prayer suggestion

Thank God for all that gives your life security and purpose, and pray for those who care for people who are blind or have other visual impairments.

For discussion

What part does guilt play in the way you behave?

Courageous faith

So he hurried down and... stood there.
LUKE 19:6, 8

He could feel their fierce gaze boring into his back. He did not need to turn to them to see the glares. They were making their feelings known. A low murmur had become a full-throated snarl.

He had not intended this to happen. It had come as such a surprise, the last thing he expected. He had not wanted to be noticed, just to observe. He wasn't the type to get involved.

He was interested to realize, though, that he had not lost his agility. It was years since he had climbed a tree. His bare feet would grip the rough bark and, with a few swings and springs, he'd be high in the leaves. But with maturity and status came a certain demeanour; with wealth and a position in the city came the need to keep one's distance. He had become skilled at protecting himself from his victims by affecting an air of powerful indifference. He had learnt that from the Roman militia: never look in the eye of the people you consider disposable. And no more tree-climbing.

If you act as if people no longer count, they soon get the message. Do it often enough to them, and they gradually become what you want them to be—worthless in their own eyes. His disdain had taught them their rightful place as people on the edge, in the margins, people fit for the drains, people who didn't count even with God.

There were always the ones who had too much to say, but he had found ways of silencing them. A casual walk through the street with the local garrison commander showed where the strength really lay. He believed in it: wealth plus superior weapons could always control the masses.

But now, with his back turned to the crowd, he could hear those noisy ones. They seemed to have lost their inhibitions. He recognized their voices, and vowed to deal with them later. This was all more than he had bargained for. He was a fool—he could at least have responded to the teacher's invitation more discreetly. It had caught him unprepared. Here he was in the midst of a hostile crowd, accepting an invitation to offer an invitation to his own house!

He was unnerved by his own delight. What was happening to him? It was as if he no longer knew himself. The little rich man had become the tiny rich fool! He had just wanted to watch what went on: he was not the type to get involved.

Now he heard the word he hated most: 'sinner'! He knew it was true: the elders of the synagogue had made his position quite clear. He could take it from them—but not from those who were tarred with the same brush. What gave them the right to speak in that way? Who was the greater hypocrite? This was all getting too much. He had just wanted to see what all the fuss was about. He was *not* the type to get involved!

So he knew he would have to come clean. There was no point him coming over all religious. The watching crowd would scoff even more. He was accepting the invitation. After all, it wasn't coming from him! He could always say that he was just being hospitable.

Yet it was more than that. It was as if he had found something within himself that had been lost. Could he still bring out the ability to be generous? Was that what he was really being asked?

For reflection

Read Luke 19:1–10. Place yourself beside the crowd, and then Zacchaeus, and explore how you would have reacted to the circumstances.

Prayer suggestion

Pray for people whose values have been compromised in some way by their employment.

For discussion

Are 'good works' the product or the cause of a new relationship with God? (See verse 10.)

Resurrection rendezvous

But Mary stood weeping outside the tomb.
JOHN 20:11

They did not stop to speak to her. She had gone early to the tomb, found it open and told the other disciples. Two of them responded instantly, racing each other to the place. Both peered into the place where the body of Jesus had been laid. They discovered that it was not just open, but empty—and neither of them talked to her.

It was as if, for that moment, Mary Magdalene did not count. They came; they saw; they left. Mary was not included, not consulted as to what they should do next.

Grief makes us do strange things. It can turn companions into acquaintances and friends into strangers. It is blind to other people's need. It can be selfish and heartless. Men and women may experience it differently. The conventions of mourning can put a distance between people who should be close. Even being a follower of Jesus can create difficulties as anguish and hurt battle with trust and serenity.

The grief of Peter and the other disciple gave them no time for Mary. They offered no consolation, did not take her home with them. They acted with indifference, pushing aside the bearer of news they could not cope with, resisting the implications of what she told them.

But things were about to change!

The dust settles. The rustle and fuss of their departure is over and Mary is alone. She has no fellow mourners. It is not time for a public show of grief. Dawn is the time when the world wakes to start its new day, regardless of those who have hardly slept for loss of a companion. The call of a new day can be a bitter irony. A new day—but already soured by yesterday's pain without relief. There is no consolation in such newness.

So Mary weeps, ignored, forgotten, burdened with loss and left by those who could have helped.

Silently he arrives.

His angels are now in sight. Mary is neither overawed nor impressed, in need of deeper comfort than heavenly special effects. She can say nothing different to them than she had said to the disciples: 'They have taken my Lord out of the tomb and I do not know where they have laid him.' She makes it personal: she feels responsible. The fleeing disciples have been no help, wanting nothing to do with unexpected developments. This is about her Lord and the last thing she can do for him.

She is stuck. It is the body she wants, but soon it will be too distasteful—the smell of it, the look of it. The repellent wounds will continue their vile corruption of his flesh. She cannot bear the thought of not knowing where it is. She needs to close the tomb again.

Silently he approaches.

Mary sees him, but she sees nothing new. His question is one that you would expect in such a place. It is just the sort of question a gentle person would ask—nothing exceptional. Anyone with a drop of the milk of human kindness in them would offer it to a tearful woman.

Mary hears nothing new. A gardener with time for a thoughtful word before the start of a day's work changes nothing. She is settled on what she must do. The search for the body gives her purpose. The disciples were no help; the angels did not reply; perhaps a man who looks after the plants around a tomb can help.

He speaks.

Was she already clinging or did she move to touch him? Whatever she did, he could not accept what she offered. His risen body was not hers any more than his dead body could be. Yet that early morning offered a promise and invitation.

This was no magical return. It was a journey that he had spoken of before, part of the ascent into the presence of the Father. She could no more hold him back in his risen presence than when he made his way to the cross. He was journeying into his God's future and he invited her to accept the future of God for herself.

So there would be no reburial, no flowers around the grave, no prospect of tearful anniversary visits in the future. She left the place of joyful recognition to share the future with... well, would you believe it?

The disciples did not know what to say. They had listened to Peter and his companion with growing worry and concern. It was too much to take in. Now Mary was having her say too. She sounded so confident. She hadn't bothered to wipe away the tear stains, and she reeked of burial spice, but there was laughter in her voice. It was either madness or mystery.

But what was God doing, telling a woman about a resurrection?

For reflection

Read John 20:1–18 and consider your own commitment to belief in the resurrection of Jesus.

Prayer suggestion

Thank God for the promise of eternal life and pray for anyone you know who is coping with some kind of loss.

For discussion

Why is it so difficult to 'let go', even when we are offered something better?

A puzzled Jesus

He was amazed at their lack of faith.
MARK 6:6 (NIV)

It is not often that the Gospel writers describe any emotional responses of Jesus, so when they do, it is worth noting.

This story in Mark is one of a small number of episodes from the Nazareth ministry of Jesus. He is back among his own people. His family have not moved far. His younger brothers and sisters are still about the place and there is nothing to suggest that he would not have been welcome there. Yet, in a period of unparalleled support and acclaim for Jesus in the Galilee region, Nazareth stands out as the exception. He meets unexpected resistance from the place that would have known him best.

Jesus himself provides an explanation. Prophets tend to run foul of their background, and the story of Israel's response to God's prophets is a mixed one. They were not universally popular. Think of Nathan and David, Elijah and Ahab, Jeremiah and the religious authorities of Judah. Prophets like Micah, Amos and Isaiah of Jerusalem did not mince their words. They brought an uncompromising word of the Lord to their times.

Jesus was no different, but he obviously expected a positive response from the people who had watched him develop and grow. Maybe there was a legacy of hurt and misunderstanding over the way he had treated his brothers and mother in a very uncomfortable encounter sometime earlier (Mark 3:31–35). And he certainly would not have made it any easier for himself that day in Nazareth by describing himself as an unwelcome prophet. Perhaps he realized, from that time, that faith cannot be a servant of status, wealth, upbringing or culture.

We are told in an earlier episode from his ministry in Capernaum that Jesus looked for a certain reaction to himself, which he described by the word 'faith' (Mark 2:5). He saw it in the action of the four men who helped their paralysed friend to reach Jesus, but he did not meet it in Nazareth (6:6). So what was he looking for? What needed to be present so that he could heal?

It was the sort of faith that is prepared to move away from its cultural conditioning, to accept something new in a person that we think we know because we have been familiar with them (or their family) for so long. He looked for a faith that is able to get beyond the limited understanding that 'the way we do things around here' is right and true—such that anyone who joins or returns to our community must not rock the boat of our assumptions. This faith is open to surprises and fresh possibilities, prepared to have its mind changed and ready to see the familiar and well-known in a different light.

This could not have been an easy experience for Jesus. In Matthew 11:4–5, he describes the evidence of his ministry for John the Baptist's disciples to report back to John. He points out all the good that he is bringing to the lives of the poor and needy, but then admits (v. 6) that he might be a problem for some people for that very reason.

In Nazareth, we see this problem working out. The story ends with Jesus leaving his home town (apparently for the last time), surprised at the people's lack of faith.

Mark explains, in his characteristically blunt way, that this unbelief prevented Jesus from doing any miracles there. He then softens the impression of this apparent quenching of the Spirit by referring to healings carried out through the laying on of hands—but he clearly wants to emphasize that the absence of a certain sort of openness and acceptance inhibited Jesus.

In Matthew's account (13:58), the editorial is slightly different, stating that Jesus chose not to perform miracles in Nazareth. It was a voluntary suspension of his ability, because he knew that the context would not welcome it. His miracles were not primarily about awakening faith; their purpose was to bring into sight what a person's faith in his presence had already discerned. The four friends in Mark 2 saw the authority of God in Jesus, so, when he met them, he described their perception as 'faith' and acted accordingly.

In chapter 6, though, Jesus seems to have discerned that any miracles would have made him even more of a stumbling block to his Nazareth neighbours. Miracles would simply have added to the people's confusion. So he left behind him a legacy of offence and disappointment—in the midst of signs of God's healing grace. Did he hope that those few healings would develop a faith in God's power in his absence, which had not been evident in his presence?

For reflection

Read Hebrews 11:1–3 and consider the relationship between the creative activity of God and human trust and belief.

Prayer suggestion

Thank God for the gift of your faith and pray for this gift to be received by other people.

For discussion

Do some people have more faith than others, or is it that they just have more boldness?

'Gospel encounters' link to 'Faith companions'

The gospel works at depths that we do not recognize until behaviour begins to change. Its hidden work may go on for a long time before it surfaces in a moment of delight, change and sacrifice.

I find I am compelled to believe this, in order to be sustained in my life as a pastoral minister. I am not called to judge others by the behaviour they adopt when we meet. I am called to believe that they are a work of God in progress, that I am privileged to meet for a brief or longer period of time. I do not know when the gospel will complete its work in them: I cannot discern that for myself.

I have found it helpful to think of God desiring to have a conversation with each one of us (1 John 4:9–10). This means that when we meet a person, we become part of a three-way conversation that has been initiated by God. As a Christian, I am therefore not to obstruct that desire of God in any way. Instead, knowing that that is what God wishes to do with me, I am called to help facilitate this conversation.

Each of the people we have considered in the last section travelled more lightly as a result of meeting Jesus: unburdened of a cloak, chains, reputation and so on. Sometimes he left them and went on his way; at other times they followed him and joined the companions of faith that surrounded our Lord.

Faith companions

The faith of the marginal

Keeping their distance, they called out.
LUKE 17:12–13

In this part of his Gospel, Luke is examining what it takes for a person to accept or reject Jesus. The answer in this healing parable is, 'it depends on the position you take'.

The ten with leprosy knew their place. They kept their distance, isolated and out of reach. They were nothing else but lepers—a horrid-sounding word for a horrid disease. It's a word that describes a category, not a person, and it is rightly falling out of use today.

We are told nothing about them, only what they suffered from. Their condition defined them, created the borders of their life, forming an exclusion zone around them. They are within sight and sound in the story but beyond reach.

Jesus too knows his place. He does not approach them. He stays put, for he is already on difficult territory. A Galilean Jew, he walks a border with Samaritan territory which, from his earliest days, he would have been warned not to enter. He is in neither one place nor another. He is 'outside the camp' and beyond the houses where others can be safe and secure.

The disciples also know their place, and it is not where Jesus has taken them! Jesus has done this before. He took them to Caesarea Philippi, a place of pagan worship (Mark 8:27–30). He went down to the coast, where they met a Syro-Phoenician woman who gave him a very difficult time (Mark 7:24–30). It seems to have been Jesus' policy to introduce his disciples to experiences and questions that were new, different and challenging. Why did he do this? Why did he take them to the edge of their world? Here are some answers.

- Going to the edge gives us a glimpse of something different.
- Walking on the borders allows us to look in and out of a situation.
- Going to the edge enables us to become a connection, a conductor for what is out of reach at the centre.
- On the margins we are less in control, less certain of ourselves, more ready to learn.

Then the healing starts. In a cleverly constructed account, Luke uses three different words to describe what happened. The lepers are 'made clean' (17:14): Jesus releases them from the taboo of their disease so that they can rejoin society, family and synagogue. They are healed: the signs of ill health are no longer visible or distressing. But to only one of them can Jesus declare that he is 'made well' (v. 19). This is total transformation. This is an experience of harmony and integrity—a person no longer fragmented and out of sorts but at one with God, creation and self.

But the encounter takes an ominous turn. The one who is on his knees in a position of worship is a Samaritan (v. 16). It would be easy to miss this seemingly innocuous piece of information, were it not for Luke's continual references in his Gospel to the marginalized and the faith of the stranger.

The Samaritans were renegade Jews. They believed that Mount Gerizim (not the temple mount) was God's holy mountain (John 4:20). They respected only the first five books of the Hebrew scriptures. Their origins were among the people who married non-Jewish colonists during the exile. For this they had suffered rejection by other Jewish tribes and clans. This was a blood feud that had gone on for centuries.

Nothing in this man would recommend itself to the background of Jesus and his disciples, except his need. As the other nine go on their way to the priest, he rushes to Jesus. He can no longer use his illness to hide his religious and cultural identity. Among the people with leprosy, he had a place. Where he had come from, what he believed, where he worshipped had not mattered. Why worry about that when an infectious disease kept you away from your critics but gave you companions in ill health?

He has nowhere to go but to Jesus. He is left behind by his erstwhile friends, who are ready to follow the path of their orthodoxy. He stands with the one who has nowhere to lay his head, the Christ who acts as the priest, going outside the camp to declare the healing done (Leviticus 14:1–3). The man seeks more from the one who has healed his body—what can he do about his past, his culture, his position in society? Jesus does not mention any of that, but simply tells him that his trust has given him the freedom of being well.

He would live on among his people, but be able to speak of an enemy who had healed him. Two enemies became friends because each was prepared to walk on the edges of what was acceptable. A Samaritan, a representative of an apostate people, was able to see God at work for him in Jesus, despite his lack of suitable qualifications. Jesus welcomed the faith of the apostate because he was prepared to transcend it.

With his true identity revealed, he and Jesus create a prophetic community, one that challenges the conventions and traditions of both Jewish and Samaritan worlds.

In Jesus, we see that God will not dwell 'within the camp'. God will not stay where we place our tent, temple, shrine, mausoleum, sanctuary, chapel or church. God will not reside in the certainties, correct language and proper belief that can inhibit us as much as shelter us.

The others were only following orders! They did what Jesus told them, which was the correct procedure, according to the rituals of purification. There seemed no joy in it, though—at least, none that they cared to share with Jesus. They may have been doing the right thing but it was not the complete picture. That day a choice was made: some were made better; one was made whole.

For reflection

Compare this story with the one in Acts 10:1–35 and consider what they both suggest about the sort of community created by the Spirit of Jesus.

Prayer suggestion

Pray for anyone you know who feels pushed out by their church.

For discussion

What is needed for a church community to reflect the impartiality of God?

Toxic religion

They realized that he was speaking about them.
MATTHEW 21:45

Although I don't always enjoy what they have to say, I am often grateful, even relieved, when people speak their mind. Sometimes I wish that they appreciated the value of tact a little more, but directness can have a cleansing effect.

I am easily irritated by conversations that seem to be about one thing when I know they are actually about something else. I try to remember that some people find it easier to approach a delicate matter by starting with another issue that will take them there by a longer route. Sometimes, however, what needs to be said needs to be said so that the air can be cleared.

Jesus was famous for using parables. The record shows that, occasionally, he left people wondering 'What was all that about?' but he told his disciples that they would always get the full interpretation, while others would need parables. In the last few days before his death, though, Jesus did not mince his words. His meaning was plain. His prophetic spirit rose high above the mean, self-serving professional religious leaders of his people and he dropped truth on them from a great height, like a stone!

When Jesus told the parable of the vineyard in Matthew 21:33–46, there was no need for him to decode it for the benefit of his listeners. They knew the meaning: it was right there in Isaiah 5. God's vineyard, his people, were not producing what was expected. All God's care and attention were being wasted. Jesus took this Old Testament song of God's unrequited love and reshaped it using contemporary events. People in his day knew all about absentee landlords, and the perceptive ones among them wondered whether the now-silenced voices of Israelite prophets had been God's way of seeking to call people back to him.

Jesus develops the scenario to the point of absurdity. The tenants are completely out of order and the story becomes darker and darker. The death, destruction and condemnation are relentless. There is no relief.

His listeners get the message. Some—those who have the most to lose and the most to sort out—want to do away with Jesus. The majority know a prophet when they hear one, and their silent approval stems the chief priests' and Pharisees' tide of religious intolerance for a while. But distorted priorities in high places always have ways and means of making themselves felt.

As I read and prayed through this parable, I found, to my surprise, that I wanted the landowner to forgive his tenants. But this would not have been consistent with the facts of the matter in first-century Palestine, or would not have taken into account the way that toxic religion needs to be dealt with. A poisoned system needs a strong response. It needs treatment that is direct, powerful and invasive. Toxic religion needs such treatment. It is:

- proud and self-deluding.
- cancerous and self-feeding.
- intolerant of outsiders.
- lacking in generosity.
- oppressive of the gullible.
- forgetful of its true nature.

These are the deadly symptoms of unhealthy spirituality. Jesus recognized religious abuse when he saw it in the public face of his religious community. It was there in the way lives were lived and temple worship was conducted, together with the daily compromises with Roman authority. As he told the parable, Jesus could look up and see the fortifications of Rome's Antonia fortress, built close to the temple wall. The rule of military power loomed over the symbol of God's power. He condemned the Pharisees for losing sight of the grace of God, in the name of control and order. He felt that, in their hands, the faith of his ancestors had lost a sense of the call of God.

A toxic religion lives only for itself. It feeds on itself—and the people called to be a light to the Gentiles were concerned only with their own path.

For reflection

Read Ephesians 2:1–22 and consider Paul's explanation of how God in Christ has tackled toxic religion.

Prayer suggestion

Consider whether you have strayed into the ways of toxic religion and pray for guidance back into the light of God's presence.

For discussion

Where are the features of toxic religion seen in the life of the churches you know, and how can they be tackled?

The faith of the questioner

Thomas said, 'Unless I see... I will not believe.'
JOHN 20:25

How do people at your church treat its sarcastic questioners? Maybe you don't know who they are. Sometimes doubt and scepticism are frowned upon. There is an unspoken discouragement. Such behaviour is just not expected or allowed, so those who have doubts and questions about what is believed or asserted keep it to themselves. They do not want to break cover because they know they will not get a sympathetic response.

Sometimes they may come up to the preacher or the person who has led the prayers and hint obliquely that what was said related to their need for help with the whole issue of belief. But the approach never seems to go much further. They may be put off by the hushed tones in which 'losing one's faith' is discussed, by the way it is treated like a disease. They notice that people shake their heads wonderingly when someone leaves the church because they have 'lost their faith', as if it were some kind of crime against the fellowship. So they keep their own counsel and do not admit that they really don't subscribe to what everyone else seems to find so apparent.

Of course, there are some who are braver. They are known to have a questioning frame of mind. But how well are they integrated into your church? Sometimes such people seem to have a no-go zone around them. They are like a farm infected by some dread disease: the notices have gone up and the equivalent of antiseptic foot wash is laid out around them. Their fearless questioning sometimes enlivens a church meeting but at other times they just seem tedious, in perpetual spiritual adolescence.

This is a valid phase for us all to undergo as we make our way through life with a faith. Sometimes we can be held in the experience of questioning far longer than we wish, or we may find that it comes upon us much later in life than we imagine it should.

One couple I knew made their difficulties very clear to me. They told me that they had come to the church for the sake of their children, and now that the children had left home, they were wondering why they still came. They felt that they had put their own faith at the back of the shelf, and did not know whether it was worth bothering about any more.

For yet other sceptics, there is at least one specific nagging doubt that they just can't get past. It looms over them as a threat. They may actually want to make headway with their Christian experience but the 'U' word always kicks in, just when they appear to have made a break through: '*Unless* I... have the answer to the question that I really want addressed, then no matter how much else I may understand and believe, I do not feel I am really a Christian.'

Do you know the sort of person I'm talking about? Does your church treat them in the way the disciples treated Thomas? It must have been a real dampener on their spirits when Thomas turned up late. Jesus had just appeared in all the glory and surprise of his resurrection. He had transformed their frightened, despairing isolation into a mood of hope and anticipation.

Thomas arrives and they rush to tell him, but he will have none of it. How easy it would have been for the other disciples to keep at a distance—but this does not happen, for we are told that when Jesus next appears, Thomas is with them.

This was a fellowship of disciples that embraced the awkward questioner. Thomas speaks up for those who need to know more and need to know for themselves. They are not prepared to rely on 'holy hearsay'. Ardent Christian witness is no substitute for careful explanation, backed up by thought-out reasons.

I have usually taken Jesus' words in John 20:29 to be spoken only to Thomas. I now wonder whether they were offered to the rest of the disciples through Thomas. Jesus was commending them for keeping in their company a person who had needed more time and opportunity to come to a deeper faith.

Not only had the disciples kept Thomas as one of their number despite his scepticism, but Thomas had wanted to remain with them despite his questioning. What an extraordinary church—a company where convinced believer and questioning agnostic had room for each other! I believe this to be one of the more important missionary tasks for our time: to create churches of honest questioning and faith, which are not afraid of faithful sceptics.

Sometimes we think that our doubts are insurmountable obstacles to our faith, when in fact they contain the seed of faith, alive and ready to grow. Those seeds of questioning faith may be just what a church needs. It was from one such faithful questioner, Thomas, that the first words of Easter praise in John's Gospel were uttered. The rest of the disciples were dumb before the risen Lord, while the worship of the convinced sceptic gave us the words of rejoicing: 'My Lord and my God!' (v. 28).

For reflection

Read Ecclesiastes 3:11 and consider whether this is an adequate description of the humility that is required to believe in God.

Prayer suggestion

Pray for those who are oppressed by questions for which they can find no answers.

For discussion

Are doubts and questions necessary for a living faith?

The power of myth

But he passed through the midst of them and went on his way.
LUKE 4:30

I am in the process of planning a video of life in my present church to use with new members. It will describe the way in which we have responded as a church to the guidance and inspiration of God. It will recall the great celebrations and painful disturbances that have shaped us.

Each church has its story. It is there in the people, who live their story through what they remember. Sometimes, what is *not* remembered tells you the story more clearly: the previous minister, who is never mentioned; the time when there was a split (now rarely talked of but probably still very real for those who were involved). In contrast, there are some features that are always recalled: the occasion when a visiting preacher, to illustrate a point, stood on one of the special chairs set aside for the person who presides at Holy Communion—or when the minister and her husband put up ladders to the gallery in the Christmas carol service. What that was all about is beyond me, but it is a favourite memory of a certain group in my present church!

Over time, such details of the church's story can develop into a myth that sustains a congregation. A myth is more than facts; it is the meaning of the facts amplified, rearranged and coloured by experience. Each congregation lives its own myth. Events and people take on a significance that helps the church explain its direction and meaning. Sometimes, what actually happened is lost, but the myth of what happened continues to be lived out. A myth, then, gives identity, shapes values, brings the past into the present and is very hard to shift from its place of control.

During my early days in Bath, there was an elderly woman who had been in domestic service all her life, from the first decades of the 20th century. She adamantly insisted on coming to evening worship rather than the morning service. That was when people in her line of work and at her level of Bath society were 'allowed' to worship. It was factually true once, but for her it had taken on a deeper significance. She knew her place in the church. She was not to be shifted. She lived her own myth.

I understand now why we call our religious buildings by different names: temple, cathedral, chapel, sanctuary, mausoleum or shrine. Each of these words describes not only the function of the space but also what the people who use the words want from the space.

I have met some Christians who really feel that they are worshipping among their ancestors. They can remember where their long-gone relatives sat in the church, even though they are no longer in view. They are living the myth of their congregation. It is powerful, meaningful and potentially dangerous.

The congregation's myth can exert a deep influence that makes things difficult for new arrivals. I hope we have moved on from the days in which to sit in someone else's seat was deemed bad manners for anyone aspiring to join a church, but it is still the case that some churches keep people in newcomer status for too long. If we do not take time to understand the myth through which the church lives its life, a newcomer may cause an upset without realizing it—or never feel that they belong.

We see Jesus encountering this problem when he returned to Nazareth. All three synoptic Gospels reveal the struggle between Jesus and the people among whom he grew up. In Luke 4:16–30, Jesus defends his outgoing ministry by reminding his hometown folk that God is not limited to the people who bear his name. This was one local lad showing that he was not prepared to live the local culture's myth. The Lord's ecumenical spirit was too much for the villagers to cope with, and he had to move on. Although he challenged them through scripture, their narrowly focused faith could not take it. Isolation and pride had created a powerful myth that built high walls of fear.

We should not think that this issue only affects churches that have been around a long time, that are burdened by a load of historical baggage. I have met people who have been part of young, vigorous congregations but have been painfully rejected because they dared to raise questions that others felt to be inappropriate. They could no longer live the myth of the first generation, and found surprising opposition. The attitude that says, 'This is not thought/done/said here' is not merely the province of the old and staid.

We can forget that we are not called to be a fellowship of our myth but a fellowship of the Holy Spirit. The challenge of the stranger or questioner is, 'Is there a place for me in your myth?' The challenge of God is, 'Can I come in with the stranger and change your myth?'

It is hard to transform the myth of a church. Paul attempts it in his first letter to the Corinthians (1:9–17). He takes the people to the baseline of Christ and his cross, and invites them to let the cross challenge and change them. He seeks to lead them on from their parochial idea of Christ to the glorious Lord of eternity. As we know, it was not an easy transformation then, and it will not be easy now.

For reflection

Read Ephesians 2:11–22 to discover the myths that Paul was challenging in the church at Ephesus, and how he presents Christ as the answer to their power.

Prayer suggestion

Pray for the discernment that lets go what need not be remembered and remembers what should not be forgotten.

For discussion

What are the myths in your local church? Are they helpful or not?

Faith in listening

Jesus spoke up and said to him, 'Simon, I have something to say to you.'
LUKE 7:40

I was reminded recently of Mrs Merton, that awful television creation by Caroline Aherne in the 1990s. She was a painful send-up of a chat show host. At one point in the programme, she encouraged audience and guests to engage in 'heated debate'. This usually meant that some self-opinionated pensioners showed themselves up in public just for a fleeting taste of televised notoriety. 'Listen to the sound of your own voice' seemed to be the one rule.

Sadly, I was reminded of this programme as I participated in a meeting of Christians. The chairman lost control, as no one was using the convention of speaking 'through the chair'. This is not always a bad thing, but on this occasion there were some people who had decided that the loudest and and most persistent voices—theirs—were going to win the decision.

Research shows that family life no longer encourages the development of the art of conversation. People tend to communicate through a series of injunctions and statements, and whoever is left talking at the end wins! Dr Jonathan Sacks, the Chief Rabbi, has declared that conversation is the heartbeat of democratic politics. It is interesting to note that the Baptist practice of holding a church meeting where the members of a local church gather to discern the mind of Christ dates from the beginnings of the democratic revolution in the 1600s.

In our society, there is a continuing upsurge in violence against gay people and regular outbursts against vulnerable groups such as asylum seekers. Violence develops when people are no longer in touch with each other as human beings. Aggression is fed by fear and ignorance. People do not listen to each other. They do not meet to talk, so they remain unable to hear the fellow human being beyond the accent.

I think that this attitude is what Jesus was resisting when he regularly accepted invitations to meet Pharisees in their homes. He went and talked with the people who found him by turns puzzling, a threat and occasionally blasphemous. These days, we would call it 'dialogue'. Equally, he offered invitations to people like Zacchaeus. During his conversation with Jesus, Zacchaeus experienced a moment of transformation in which he saw all the rest of his life in a new light. He was no longer bound to the oppressive system that not only oppressed others but also oppressed him.

It has been said that true dialogue liberates the imagination. It allows us to dream other possibilities. It permits us to think and speak the unexpected.

Gerard Hughes, author of *God in All Things* (Hodder & Stoughton, 2003), suggests that any group studying his book should adopt a particular way of working. They should put a priority on listening to each other. This means that no one speaks a second time until everyone who wishes to has spoken for the first time. And once the first person has spoken, no one taking their turn to speak is permitted to argue with what another has said—or even to agree with it. Each person speaks solely for themselves, and all are heard. Everyone is valued for what they offer. The process may sound rather tedious, but whenever I have experienced this way of conversation I have longed for it to happen more often in meetings with fellow Christians where a decision is required. The discernment of the will of God is, I believe, a necessarily slow experience.

True dialogue occurs when our words to each other are thought of as an exchange of gifts rather than a negotiation. Surely this is what is going on in the conversation between Jesus and the Syro-Phoenician woman in Mark 7:24–30. Jesus listens; he understands;

he receives what the woman is offering and responds differently as a result.

The problem with Mrs Merton's 'heated debate' was that it would result in some winning and others feeling that they had lost the argument. When we lose an argument, it is easy to feel that we no longer belong to the community where the dispute took place. How many people do you know of, who are no longer with your church because of that kind of experience?

Originally, the meaning of the word 'conversation' was to do with living with someone, not simply talking with them. To 'converse' was to make space for a person close to you. Argument or, for that matter, discussion does the opposite. It separates; it dissects; it breaks apart rather than uniting. I am not suggesting that there is no place for a frank exchange of viewpoints, but I am suggesting that our viewpoint should be offered in open hands, as it were, rather than being dumped in the other person's lap, whether they want it or not.

Jesus, Luke 7 tells us, was at Simon the Pharisee's home, and couldn't help but notice Simon's disapproval of a woman's impassioned response to the presence of Jesus. It was probably written all over Simon's face. Jesus responds by starting up a conversation. Before he knows it, Simon is listening to a story and being drawn into talking about the woman—a subject that he wanted to avoid. Jesus left the Pharisee under no illusion. Simon's attitude needed to be confronted, but this insight was not shouted from a distance; it was offered as a gift, one that Simon was free to accept or reject.

For reflection

Read John 9. It is full of conversations; notice their effect on the people involved.

Prayer suggestion

Pray for the gift of listening.

For discussion

Would the way of a listening conversation be valuable in any of your circumstances?

Whom do you serve?

But Christ is all and in all!
COLOSSIANS 3:11

One Sunday, as she left the church, a member of my congregation whispered, 'I think there was a hint in the sermon that you will be soon leaving us.' I was slightly unnerved because (a) leaving wasn't on my mind and (b) I couldn't recognize what I might have said to provoke such a reaction. Of course, there's an even scarier thought —that my enquirer might have been setting up a sort of stalking horse that would get me going!

I have been pondering since then about the complicated dynamics of the relationship between minister and congregation. The psychological tools of projection and transference open up some insight. Together, minister and congregation play out roles that they give one other, and both live with the consequences of previous years. In all my churches, I have never been very similar to my predecessors but, in each one, it has been both a burden and a blessing to be a reminder of those previous leaders for some members of the church.

There are pastoral implications in all of this. I have often recognized that, unwittingly on my part but of necessity for some people, I have acquired a sort of priestly role. This is not language that would normally be used to describe a Baptist minister, but, if part of being a priest is to represent God to others, then that is what happens to me. My use of words, the images I use, how I look as I lead worship, the sound of my voice and the theology I embrace have all become a means of enabling others to sense the presence of God. This is not a matter of the theology of priesthood; it is simply a matter of fact. Some people seem to need me so that they can feel close to God.

Now even to have written the above paragraph strikes me as extraordinarily arrogant and patronizing! I want people to take responsibility for their own faith. I long for other people and for myself to have a deep, Christ-centred trust in God the Father that absorbs the changes and chances of life in our congregation and world (Ephesians 3:14–21). I don't want to be anyone's passport to heaven. Yet it happens. It can be idolatrous for those who place such expectations in their minister, and a pernicious subversion of the minister's calling, which should come from the Lord first, not from his people.

In 1 Corinthians 3:5–14, Paul tackles one of the many problems of the troubled church community in Corinth: the idolization of its ministers. Both Apollos and Paul himself had great influence in the early days of that church, but now, Paul and Apollos have their separate groups of followers, who are not in agreement. With disputes rising and tensions caused by moral and cultural differences, the separate theologies of Apollos and Paul are being seen as solutions.

Paul's answer to this potential sectarianism is disarmingly simple. He agrees that both he and Apollos have had great influence, but he condemns the Corinthians for not giving credit where it is due. He writes, 'I planted the seed, Apollos watered it, but God made it grow' (v. 6, NIV). For Paul, Apollos and he were simply God's agents in bringing the Corinthians to faith. They had a task that they had followed through. Now the congregation had to start working it out for themselves.

Paul, of course, is not averse to giving them plenty of advice. We have no record of any correspondence from Apollos but Paul certainly kept in touch with the people. He builds in two safeguards for the community: first, the foundation is Christ, so all that is done needs to be true to Christ; second, whoever builds on that foundation must take care over what he does.

Paul is indicating that good leadership of God's people is about stability. Leaders should not be profligate with the gifts of God and his people. They should not try to take over God's role. They need to be able to withstand the scrutiny of God's loving judgment. People are precious creations. Their faith in Jesus is a gift, and they need to discover that it is deeply valuable. With that gift, God moves mountains. It must not become flawed by human pride or fear. A congregation must not become a preacher's clique, a worship leader's following, or a haven for clergy-groupies.

Members of a congregation are not servants of the minister or the denomination. They are not anyone's statistical return. They are a work of God—though still with a lot of room for improvement, of course. What a release is offered by this perspective! If, as Paul suggests, a church is like a garden or a building (v. 9), there may be much to do in it, but it is God's energy that brings the transformation.

For reflection

Read 1 Corinthians 1:10–31 and explore the characteristics of the foundation in Christ that Paul wishes to build upon.

Prayer suggestion

Pray for churches that are divided against themselves.

For discussion

Why do clergy-groupies exist?

An attractive church

'Go therefore and make disciples... baptizing... and teaching.'
MATTHEW 28:19–20

In the Declaration of Principle of the Baptist Union of Great Britain, it is stated that it is the duty of every disciple to bear witness to the gospel of Jesus Christ and take part in the evangelization of the world.

Recently, my attention has been drawn back to this basis of our Union for a number of reasons. For instance, I agree with those who say that there is a general lack of confidence among many churchgoers, and I think it is a lack of confidence in the gospel. Maybe it is because many people are just churchgoers, and that's all. They have no personal witness apart from what they do on a Sunday morning, and not always every Sunday at that.

I remember a conversation with ministry colleagues during my time in Wales, back in the 1970s. We were talking about the changing patterns of Sunday service observance. One of us remarked that in the early years of the century many church members would attend twice on a Sunday and also be involved in Sunday school on a Sunday afternoon. This amounted to at least three periods of sustained Christian teaching. My colleague acknowledged the draw-backs of this level of involvement—the negative consequences for family life—but went on to comment dryly, 'These days people come once on a Sunday, expect no more than 20 minutes' teaching and think that will build healthy Christian lives. Pastoral experience suggests that it is no improvement on what we did years ago.'

I notice, however, that even among many conscientious Christians there is a lack of confidence in the gospel. We struggle to believe that the message of salvation in Jesus Christ will transform lives in our society. This lack of confidence manifests itself in various ways. Some people will correctly state that we should be known by the fruit of our lives: our actions count. But the inference seems to be that personal witness does not need to include a verbal expression of what we believe. Another way that people avoid the issue is to point to a form of evangelism that they do not agree with, suggest that that is the only way evangelism can be done, and therefore declare that they are against it! We are in danger of losing the gift of faith-sharing. Personal witness is about actions speaking louder than words, but it is also about our words interpreting our actions.

I think there may be another reason for our hesitancy. Could it be that many of us have no clear reason for calling others to faith in Christ? We are, in fact, practising universalists, even though we may not publicly deny the uniqueness of Christ.

In the journal of his sabbatical completed only a few weeks before his death in 1996, the Roman Catholic writer Henri Nouwen speaks of meeting an evangelical group called The Gathering in Cancun, Mexico. They devoted their considerable wealth to the care of others, seeking to open up opportunities to explain the ways of God in Christ. The encounter had left him pondering his own approach to mission, conversion and witness. He declared that, in all honesty, he struggled with their conviction that without an explicit personal profession of faith in Jesus as our Lord and Saviour, we cannot make it to heaven.

Nouwen went on to describe his own convictions about what it means to share faith with people who do not have it. He believed that a personal experience of the transforming power of the gospel created a desire for others to have a life-changing experience of the Lord. He was clear that if people are not left pondering their relationship with God through their encounter with us, we have not served them well.

I gave my life to the Lord Jesus Christ when I was seven years old. It was during a special service for the Sunday school anniversary. I sat among dozens of boys and girls of my own age and realized that

Jesus was very important. He had achieved something for us that I would not be able to do for myself. It was therefore necessary for him to become the centre of my life.

Of course, at that age I am not sure what life I anticipated having in the future. I was only seven and could have had little sense of what I would have to face. But my decision was treated with absolute seriousness by people in the church. I do not remember any minister being involved. My Sunday school teachers were a carpenter and a Post Office worker; the Boy's Brigade officers were a funeral director and architect's draughtsman, and the leaders of the Christian Endeavour youth group were a secretary and a factory worker. They told me more about Jesus and offered what they could from the life of the church, and eventually they and I confirmed my childhood's decision by baptism when I was 14.

I left that church in my 20s, but those early beginnings were God's gift to me. They are also a living exposition of Matthew 28:18–20 (what some call the Great Commission). Jesus gives three tasks to his small group of followers. They are to make disciples, baptize them in the name of the Trinity and teach all that Jesus said. My childhood experience of church reflects that pattern. My faith was fashioned by the willingness of others to give me their time. They told the stories of Jesus. They informed me and argued with me. They lived the Christian life and they expected me to respond. They waited for and welcomed my choice of baptism as a believer.

In the Gospels, there is no record of the coming of the Spirit upon the disciples. They are given an educational mission: their evangelism is to take the form of education. The words of the Great Commission suggest something like a form of synagogue: communities of learning and gathering, where cleansed lives could be enriched with the presence of the Saviour and where the life of Jesus would be remembered and embraced. His presence would become self-evident as his teaching was explored and explained. It was in the commandments he taught during his earthly ministry that Jesus would be present with his disciples and establish his rule among all nations.

These Christian synagogues would not be exclusive but would be created among every race, people and group. They could not grow unless disciples of one culture entered another and lived their discipleship in strange surroundings. From the beginning of each one, there would have to be a mingling of opposites.

Fundamentally, Matthew 28 is not so much a call to be mission-minded as a command to become a community of disciples, thereby attracting others to become disciples of Jesus. The Great Commission describes their nature and their cause. Wherever Jesus' followers were, they could become a company of disciples centred on the word of Christ, and wherever there was water there could be baptism. This is a vision of the Church that can be planted in any culture and at any time.

For reflection

Read Hebrews 13 for a further description of a Christian synagogue.

Prayer suggestion

Pray for guidance for ways in which you can share your faith.

For discussion

What does a Christian need in order to talk naturally about what their faith means to them?

Where is your church?

Gaius, who is host... to the whole church, greets you.
ROMANS 16:23

When people discover I live in Bath, they ask, 'Where is your church?' Sometimes I wonder whether it is a way of finding out more about me or discovering what they might get involved with, if they turn up one day. I usually say that we are just up from the railway station, across from the bus station and next door to the police station. We are nothing if not well served and noticeable. But, really, that's only *where* we are for a couple of hours a week.

It would be better if I said, 'Well, right now some of us are probably at home preparing a meal; quite a number will be keeping appointments at their GP's surgery and at least three are in hospital recovering from operations. We are teaching in all styles of school, lecturing at university, and travelling to business meetings, somewhere on the motorway system. There are always some of us going away on a short break or returning from one. We are grandparents supporting the extended family, friends doing shopping for our neighbours, pupils in the playground and students in front of the computer screen. Some of us are helping out in the church coffee shop or the local care home.'

To answer in that way would be to treat seriously the words of Paul in both Romans 12 and 1 Corinthians 12. The church is where the gifts of Christ's people are being put to work as his body, alive and active in the world. The gifts of the Spirit emerge from everyone in the body of the church, wherever they are offered and placed at the disposal of God. That service may be offered within our building at certain times, but most of the time we are dispersed: as 'toes', 'ears' and 'eyes' of Christ's body, we are creating connections for God in our restless, disoriented world.

Of course, the question may be asked in a different way: not '*Where* is your church?' but 'Where is your *church*?' They are wondering what type of church I belong to. In that case, remembering the words of Jesus in John 10:16, I may need to answer differently, for my church is not composed just of Baptist people. When I pray for my church, I always pray for another local church in the centre of Bath to remind myself that God is seeking to work his will through all Christians. 'Being church' today is no longer about 'me in my small corner and you in yours'. I am very aware, from my own congregation, that for some of us our church is not simply what goes on at our Manvers Street building. We are involved in networks and gatherings that help us express our worship and witness in different ways, such as the YMCA, Baptist Peace Fellow-ship, Iona Community, and Churches Together in Bath. Some of our members worship at Evensong in Bath Abbey or seek silence in a local monastery.

It has been suggested that over 40 per cent of all Christians now have no connection with a local church. For all sorts of reasons, people draw on the riches of Christ beyond the patterns of church shaped by the needs and expectations of previous generations. I do not know whether to be daunted, disappointed or thrilled by this trend, but I recall the words of Jesus when faced with the zealous prejudice of some of his disciples: 'Anyone who is not against us is for us'.

I find that a challenging idea in a time when the local church often seems to be downgraded in people's ranking of what is effective for the kingdom of God. Today's multi-choice, customized culture, in which my needs and expectations must be available on call, can lead to a selfish exclusivity. On the other hand, there are currently some exciting explorations of new ways of 'being church'—responsive to what is going on now, and unafraid of being provisional. They are the church for travellers that Jesus called into being for his disciples in their ministry together, a church that travels light and is energized by the mission of Christ (Mark 6:7–13).

The question may come, 'But where is *your* church?' If it is put like that, I have to reply, 'It is where my heart is.' Jesus tells us that where our treasure is—all that enriches and delights and gives life to us—that is what will capture our hearts. Since church is the body of Christ, it is far more than a box made of bricks or the group of people whom I like or who will tolerate me. Church is not simply all that we may do in the name of Jesus. It is given—a gift of grace, a fellowship of the Holy Spirit in the making. It is God's life breathed into our clay, a people for God. This is the work of God and it is wonderful to witness.

For reflection

Read any of the scripture passages mentioned above and consider what they reveal about being church.

Prayer suggestion

Thank God for the churches that have been part of your faith journey.

For discussion

So where is your church?

The age of the Spirit

'In the last days it will be, God declares, that I will pour out my Spirit upon all flesh'
ACTS 2:17 (QUOTING JOEL 2:28)

It was such a pleasure to sit on the back row. I was at the annual Christian Aid Week service in Bath. The local United Reformed Church was playing host and a rather disappointing number from a few churches spread themselves out evenly to give the visiting preacher a sort of welcome. I took advantage of having no speaking role to claim the back seat, noticing that some of our usual back row huggers were nearer the front than usual!

The service was sturdy, well planned and well prepared, but it had to carry the weight of a design with 'one-size-fits-all' in mind. It was Pentecost Sunday evening, and I rather arrogantly wondered whether the only tongues of fire were to be of the silver foil variety hanging from the balcony! My path to a humbler frame of mind commenced with the reading of Acts 2:1–21. As if I had never heard it before, the soaring declaration of the prophet Joel cut through my jaded professionalism.

At the beginning of the Church era, the first words that we hear from the Old Testament come not from one of the Hebrew headline prophets but from one deemed to be a minor prophet, and probably Division Two at that—a sort of Torquay United among the Chelseas and Arsenals. Little Joel is an obscure voice sandwiched between the terrible two, Micah and Amos. He goes on about locusts and lamentation, but he is used by Peter to explain the roaring, surging force of the Holy Spirit bringing to birth the new people of God. His words fitted the time. He is not heard again in the New Testament. Joel is the prophet of Pentecost.

He speaks from a time of transformation for Israel. The great days of prophecy are over. He borrows from Ezekiel and Obadiah. His words throb with expectancy and severe mercy as he longs for the Day of the Lord—a day that will involve cosmic reorientation and an unprecedented outpouring of the Spirit of God.

For Peter, Joel's time has come. The fickle disciple who found new courage in the Spirit sees the massed crowds of pilgrims. He overhears their amazement as they recognize the actions of God described in their own languages. He notices the puzzlement of the embarrassed scoffers, ready to laugh off the antics of his fellow disciples as the result of an early morning 'happy hour', and he nervously realizes that there is more going on than that! Peter sees faith-history happening before his very eyes.

Joel says what Peter sees: young, old, slaves, men and women all infectiously responding to the new act of God in Jesus. This is finale time! What more can God do than break out of one place, one time and one faith and bless his world with the knowledge of his presence? Yet Peter is ready to silence Joel too. Compare what Joel originally said and you will notice that Peter does not confirm the prophet's hope that Jerusalem will be the place of rescue. Peter cannot limit himself to the vision of the restored Israel.

Many hundreds of years later, I too heard the words of Joel as I slumped in the back seat of a Bath church. They transformed the scene. I too realized that I live in their fulfilment. There were not many slaves in sight, admittedly, but all the other categories mentioned in Joel were present. Some had walked many miles collecting money during successive Christian Aid weeks. The vision and the dream of that charity had not dimmed since the early years after World War II. Some workers there were able to remember Christian Aid's first birthday. Some of the old men present were still living their dreams.

A singing group led us in the anthem of the defeat of apartheid from South Africa: 'We are marching in the light of God'. I was reminded of a time when all we had was a dream that one day that land would be free of its oppression. It's no longer a dream, but a reality!

Earlier in the week, I had been part of a consultation called by Churches Together in England. We were asked to explore what might be signs of healthy and unhealthy spirituality in contemporary experience. It was a hard task but we could not deny that we live in a spiritual age. Some are calling it a time of spiritual revolution. It is certainly a time when Christians need to explore with deepening enthusiasm the work of the Spirit of God among all flesh. The Spirit begins his work in the lives of all people. This then becomes a sign for the followers of Christ. God is always at work in our world, always doing surprising and important things. He is a God who sows the seeds of the Spirit, and we are called to share in the growth and the change that will come as a result of his compassionate activity among us.

For reflection

Read Revelation 21:1–5, 22–27 with its vision of universal fulfilment.

Prayer suggestion

Ask God to help you see the world as a place of the Spirit's activity.

For discussion

Do we conceive of the work of the Spirit too narrowly when we limit his activity to the life of the church?

'Faith companions' link to 'Praying the gospel'

They may annoy me or puzzle me. They may be people I have known for a very long time or just met in passing. They may speak with my accent or pronounce well-loved words of faith in a strange way. But they are all the people who have been part of my faith journey. It is not for me to question why they have come into my life. I need to believe that, with them, God is using me to create a community of belief that honours his Son.

At the heart of that community is one prayer—a prayer that compels me to think beyond myself. It is the prayer of all Christians. Have you noticed that there is no past tense in the Lord's Prayer, save one? Everything in the prayer is about the present and the future; its direction is forward-looking. The requests for the present time are at the service of our journey into the future of the kingdom of God. This is a prayer for an Easter faith.

Everything around us may be changing. We may have real concerns about the future of our church. We cannot see how the gospel will draw the heart and mind of our godless, self-absorbed culture. We struggle to make our worship a sign of contemporary faith rather than a commemoration of previous generations' belief. The Lord's Prayer is the antidote to such Christian pessimism. We are always journeying into a future with God.

This is a prayer that lives the resurrection now. It has an infectious energy, challenging anything that deals in death or limitation. Its horizon is the kingdom, power and glory of God. Its destiny is the will of God being done on earth. Its desire is that the righteousness of God be given respect and honour. Its focus is the intimate nature of God revealed in the relationship that Jesus shared with his Father in heaven. Throughout, this prayer advances into God's future. It is a prayer for all times and all places.

This prayer gave Jesus' disciples their identity. It was his prayer given to them, an offering of the discoveries of his prayer life to his followers. I cannot help but think that this is what Luke is suggesting when he describes the disciples coming to Jesus for instruction while he was 'praying in a certain place' (11:1). This vivid episode reflects the hope in that other prayer in John 17, where the Lord asks that his disciples be absorbed into the relationship of the Father and the Son.

Jesus was not giving his disciples a form of words to follow. He was offering an experience—his experience of God. The words are what we need, but they are merely vehicles that carry us into the presence of God. So this is a prayer to be digested slowly. It is not simply a format, to be tucked into an appropriate part of a service or used as a tidy-up in our own devotions—although when all other words dry up, simply praying this prayer can be helpful. The words of the Lord's Prayer can speak for us in the Spirit. Are they not the sighs of his Spirit?

Praying the gospel

His prayer is our prayer

'Pray then in this way.'
MATTHEW 6:9

In both Matthew 6 and Luke 11, Jesus is commenting on the prayer life of others. He offers what has been rightly called the Disciples' Prayer, as well as the Lord's Prayer, for prayer is at the heart of a disciple's relationship with God. These words from Jesus can shape our prayer and guide our life. They are more than just his words for us to pray. Through them, Jesus offers his relationship with the Father to us. To name God as Father has consequences for our priorities and lifestyle.

This prayer also offers us our Lord's own discipleship class. Many ancient parish churches inscribed the Lord's Prayer on their walls alongside the Ten Commandments. The prayer is a core text for a gospel lifestyle. It defines the Church of Christ as much as the Commandments defined God's people of Israel.

When I was on my travels as Baptist Union President, I noticed how rarely the prayer was used in the church services I attended. This rather surprised me. Did leaders fear that its regular use each Sunday would turn it into a heap of empty phrases (Matthew 6:7)? Or were the churches unable to decide whether to use the traditional words or one of the contemporary versions, and so gave up its use altogether? Or is it that the Baptist preference for heartfelt extempore prayer makes people unsure whether the words have a sufficiently contemporary ring to them? (If so, no amount of use will change that perception.)

These may be legitimate concerns, but they do not mean that we should neglect the value of this prayer for a Christ-like life. Certainly, in my own church I am told that we need variety in its use. When we use it in every service, at the same part of the service, it is very easy to go on to auto-pilot as we say it. So I do vary its use—not just so that we are kept alert but because the point of the Disciples' Prayer is too important to allow it to be swamped by boredom.

I justify my use of the prayer in our worship by looking at the context of the two versions that we find in the Gospels. In Matthew 6, it appears in a collection of Jesus' teachings on prayer. He explores the motivation and style of prayer in the life of his disciples, and then offers this model of Christian prayer. It is succinct; it has disciplined brevity to it. It is clearly a community prayer, with a rhythm that would allow it to be spoken by more than one voice together. Matthew has his readers' worship in mind.

In Luke 11, it is presented as the prayer from a popular rabbi, which will help to distinguish his followers from others. It is even briefer than the version in Matthew, but it confirms the allegiance of the disciples. It defines whose followers they are. Luke then adds Jesus' teaching on the importance of persistent prayer as part of our partnership with the Father. God needs the work of prayer to destroy the power of humankind's foolish entanglement with sin.

With these contexts in mind, I use Jesus' prayer at the beginning of our church worship. There I seek to use it in a Lukan way. We pray the prayer, and it brings us together. We declare whose we are and what we believe. I suppose that it almost takes on a credal significance. At other times, I use it to conclude our prayers of intercession for the world. Often, this is the part of our worship where we stumble against the many contradictions and struggles involved in what it means to desire the will of God for his creation. It feels good to conclude our incoherent groaning with the satisfying completeness of the model prayer, as Matthew intends.

There is a similar sense of completeness when we use the prayer as the offering is brought to the Lord's table. As the spiritual descendants of the disciples in Luke's account, we pledge our commitment to Jesus with its words. We are part of his people; we share faith in him together, and the prayer is our badge of allegiance.

All this is not sufficient, however. The Lord's Prayer was not intended to be kept for church on Sunday, no matter how often someone like me rings the changes in its use. I want to release this prayer from any imprisonment in our Sunday services, and I want to rescue it from redundancy caused by our desire for contemporary worship.

The prayer takes us to the heart of our Saviour and his relationship with the Father. It is the gift of Jesus for his disciples in every age.

For reflection

Compare the two Gospel settings where the Lord's Prayer was first heard. What are the distinctive features in each version? Can you explain them?

Prayer suggestion

Use the Lord's Prayer regularly, praying the words slowly and quietly asking God to guide you to their importance for you.

For discussion

What is the point of using the Lord's Prayer in an act of worship?

Praying to the Father

'When you pray, say: Father...'
LUKE 11:2

For some people, the use of the word 'Father' to describe God presents difficulties. They may not have had the best experiences of fatherhood in their lives or they may find the word too heavily loaded with images of male authoritarianism. It might soften the impact if we remember that to call God 'Father' is to use the word as a metaphor: God is something *like* a father.

This is a useful reminder about all the language we use when describing God. It is inevitably metaphorical, because we are describing the indescribable. When we treat religious language as being metaphorical, we are released from taking a literalistic attitude to the text of scripture and set free to explore the meaning of the words and their contemporary applications.

I often hear people describe God as the Father of the human race. This is not the meaning of the word in the Disciples' Prayer. God is not God the Father simply because God is our creator. God is Father because Jesus had a relationship with God. 'Father' summed up the feeling of that relationship for him so he offered the word to his disciples for their use and their exploration of God. God is most securely our Father when we join Jesus in the family circle created by his compassion and his life as a whole.

God is not Father because he has made us but because he has saved us. He has taken on all that was destroying us—fear, frustration, decay, disease and death—and put them in their place. This is the basis of Paul's powerful use of the word in Romans 8:14–16. We are able to address God as Father because of the life-changing obedience of Jesus on the cross. His voluntary death carried into oblivion all that separates us from God. The work of his Spirit now excavates a place of obedience out of the quarry of our struggles of faith.

In Matthew 11:27, Jesus explains the meaning of his speical relationship with God. He felt that the only way he could describe this relationship was by calling God 'Abba', a word used to describe a deeply respected person. A person thus called was worthy of complete loyalty and respect. I think we need to remember this when we are told that 'Abba' meant 'Daddy' on the lips of a young child. I fear that this interpretation has become so commonplace that, for some people, reverence for God has all but been replaced by the self-indulgent cosiness of a cosseted child.

The word 'Abba' was so important and exclusive for Jesus that he commanded us not to use it for anyone else in our life (Matthew 23:9). This is not a comfortable thought. Read the whole of the opening paragraph of Matthew 23 and then Mark 3:31–35 and you will start to understand the territory described by the first word in the Disciples' Prayer.

God has no rivals. God the Father of our Lord Jesus Christ has an exclusive claim on us. When we realize that, we discover that we can be more than just part of the whole family of humankind created by God. To pray to God as 'Father' is to say that our first family is not our biological family but rather the family of Christ's brothers and sisters. When we pray 'Our Father', then, we are questioning the status of the family in our culture.

For many Christians in our sort of society, this will seem difficult to accept. We may think that Christianity is about putting family first. Of course, our faith can make us better parents and help us cope with the ups and downs of living together, but there is little encouragement in the the Disciples' Prayer—or the rest of the New Testament—to make our biological family a priority over the family of the body of Christ. At certain times of need, this will need to happen, but the prayer teaches us to look beyond our families to see our membership, through baptism, in the family that has been called out from all the cultures, nations and families of the world.

It is this understanding that created the 'gathering' model of church which was so important to Christians like Baptists in the early days of their formation, many of whom did have to leave their human families and stake all on being a follower of Jesus. What we call now the Free Churches were a disturbing force in society. They challenged the Established Church, which had created parishes and sought to baptize all the residents in them. For the Free Churches, being a Christian was not only a case of where a person was born and what his or her family believed. Each person needed to consent to the identity given to them by baptism. To be baptized is to respond to the work of God's grace, which enables us to call him 'Father' regardless of our family's wishes.

We need to be warned before we go much further with the Disciples' Prayer: it can be very disturbing and challenging for our faith.

For reflection

Read the selections of scriptures noted above, as well as Ephesians 3:14–21, to explore further the New Testament view of God as 'Father'.

Prayer suggestion

Consider how you need to give priority to the various types of relationship in your life.

For discussion

Do you agree that the 'gathered' type of church best suits the notion of God as Father of a family called to be with him?

A community of prayer

Our Father in heaven, hallowed be your name.
MATTHEW 6:9

The Disciples' Prayer begins with a call into a community at prayer. When we pray these words, we have no choice but to recognize that this prayer is not our personal property—and nor is the life that it shapes.

When we follow Matthew's version of the prayer and use the word 'our', we leave our solitary Christian journey behind. 'Our Father' does not mean that God belongs to us. God is not ours to do with as we choose. God is not like our car or our family or our church. We cannot possess God. In fact, it is the other way round: God is our God because God has reached out to us. His love is the first step in our journey with this prayer. We are made for friendship with God: this is our default position.

In John 15:12–17, Jesus explains that he has created the friend-ship between us by laying down his life. We belong to him as friends, not as slaves. We are his choice. This is the undeserved and unexpected grace of divine mercy. We do not always feel like a Christian, we may not always act like one, but the choice to be a Christian was not simply ours.

What we often take to be 'our' decision to follow God is, in fact, the call of God to us to begin a journey, and it is a journey of friendship. On the way, a conversation starts. Some the words we use on this journey are uniquely ours, but not all of them. We share words in common with fellow Christian travellers, including the words of the Disciples' Prayer. They provide common ground, a shared resource for purposeful living.

In our congregation in Bath, we have people from all over the world. At our last Pentecost festival, I invited those present to pray the Lord's Prayer in their own language. It was a powerfully moving occasion in which I felt that we really did join the experience of the people in Jerusalem who said, while listening to Peter and the other disciples, 'In our own languages we hear them speaking about God's deeds of power' (Acts 2:11). The experience opened up a fresh awareness of our unity in Christ. It called us to recognize that people very different from ourselves are following the same path of Christian friendship with God. 'Ours' means 'theirs'!

I recall, very early in my days at theological college, praying the Lord's Prayer while sitting next to the college principal. I was in awe of him. As a timid 18-year-old, I felt disconcerted in his company. But as I listened to him praying the same words as I was praying, it brought him down to earth: he too was a disciple of Jesus. He may have known more than I did about scripture and the Christian faith, but when it came to the Disciples' Prayer, Jesus gave us both the same words to use!

The next phrase of the prayer turns our focus from our community and on to God himself. A new type of fraud is becoming very popular: stealing someone's identity and using it for criminal purposes. People are not just upset when this happens to them; they are outraged at a very deep level. To steal a person's identity is to commit a sacrilege. It means trespassing on the sacred ground of who we are and all that that means—and our name and identity go together. The belief that each human being is unique may have biblical roots but it is one of the unquestioned values in our society. We are hallowed beings.

In biblical theology, this deep reverence for the human being arises from our creation in the image of God. Thus, in Exodus 20:7, the prohibition on making wrongful use of God's name is not only about God; it is about our nature too. Just as our name and identity go together, so do God's. This is a commandment not to steal God's identity; it is about letting God be God. It puts negatively what Jesus says positively in the Disciples' Prayer. When we hallow the name of God, we are declaring our commitment to a certain approach to creation. The creator is not to be trivialized; the Father of our Lord Jesus Christ is not a name to be taken for granted. When we use the holy name, we are declaring what we believe about God and what we value in ourselves and his creation.

So how do we hallow the name of God?

- We hallow the name of God when our worship reflects all that is wonderful about God.
- We hallow the name of God when our answer to the question 'What is God like?' is not an embarrassed, vague stutter but a quiet assertion: 'Let's look at Jesus.' We cannot claim to hallow God's name and yet be unable to explain the impact of the Christ-like God in Jesus.
- We hallow the name of God when our lifestyle is Christ-like. We live in a time when Christians have disappeared from most people's familiar experience. Our message is not being heard, so our personal and corporate life must be lived in such a way that plausibility is restored to the Christian way.

We may be entering a time when we must wait to be rediscovered as Christ's people. In our frenetic, lung-bursting society, it is the stability and composure of our lives that will show us for whose we are. Christians are a hallowed people who belong to a hallowed God. We will be known not by our good deeds alone, but by our good hearts.

The outcome of a bad heart is described by Jesus in Mark 7:20–23. This terrible list of ugliness and depravity can reduced to one human experience: the loss of respect. Our society has at last recognized that this is our condition: there is a deep longing within us for respect. The second phrase of the Disciples' Prayer arises from the same desire for a restored world in which the honouring of the name of God goes hand in hand with the consequent respect for his supreme creation, humankind. It invites us to embrace our relationship with the Father, restored in Christ.

For reflection

Philippians 2:1–5 describes a life that hallows God in Christ.

Prayer suggestion

'May the mind of Christ my Saviour live in me from day to day, by his love and power controlling all I do or say' (Katie B. Wilkinson, 1859–1928).

For discussion

In what ways can the name of God be hallowed in our daily lives?

The focus of prayer

Your kingdom come.
MATTHEW 6:10

The kingdom of God was at the heart of the ministry of Jesus. He fought for an understanding of kingdom living in his wilderness temptations. It is there in his parables and the Disciples' Prayer. It drops into his conversations when he is defending his ministry. During his last meal before his death, he speaks of its coming. The contrite criminal dying alongside him sees in Jesus the one who can deliver to him the kingdom, and Jesus is joyfully positive in his reply.

The kingdom is not an out-of-this-world experience in which the stresses and strains of life are removed. We are to pray that the kingdom might come on earth. This is not a prayer that disengages us from the here and now, although we must recognize that any real hope for ourselves and our world that will transform the present is fuelled by a sense of purpose and direction from beyond us. This is what Jesus meant when he said, 'My kingdom is not of this world' (John 18:36, NIV). To live in the kingdom is to be sustained by energy beyond ourselves.

The kingdom of God is not the same as the church. Jesus expected his disciples to be heralds of the kingdom. While their life together might be a foretaste of the kingdom, they would always be a sign indicating its presence and its coming. In fact, however, if we begin with human activity we will not grasp the meaning of the kingdom at all, for in this part of the Disciples' Prayer (as in all the teaching of Jesus that uses this expression), he is speaking of the activity of God. The kingdom is God acting as the Lord of the universe, the king of creation, the ruler of the nations and the Saviour of our lives. The kingdom is everything that God is doing, both unseen and seen.

To pray for the kingdom to come is, according to Matthew 6:33, to give our full attention to what God requires and allow everything else to fall into place. The Disciples' Prayer suggests the same set of priorities as Jesus explores in Matthew 6:25–32: God comes first and then follows concern for our daily bread.

In this part of the prayer, the disciple is being asked to sort out priorities. Jesus is saying, 'When you pray, make sure you have a desire to know what God is doing.' We are to pray for the desire to let the glorious activity of God be our focus and hope. Jesus wants his followers to discover, deep within themselves, the conviction that even when everything seems to the contrary, God is still at work. This is the heart of prayer. It is the longing to know and share the missionary-compassion of God for his creation.

Paul writes, 'For the kingdom of God is not a matter of eating and drinking, but of righteousness, peace and joy in the Holy Spirit' (Romans 14:17, NIV). This is one of the few times when Paul talks about the kingdom of God. For Jews, the 'kingdom' described the work and purpose of God—the sovereign authority of God in action. Some Jews believed that the kingdom would be present when they had a country of their own again, which would be reminiscent of the days of David or Solomon. Others believed that the kingdom was present when a person's life was transformed by obedience and willingness to do the will of God. Paul links this idea to the universal gift of the resurrection, the Holy Spirit. For him, the kingdom is created by the power of the Holy Spirit, making a way of linking Christians today to the incarnate presence of God in Jesus in first-century Galilee. When we let the Holy Spirit lead and direct us, we will become shaped by the lifestyle and priorities of Jesus.

We may not be able to walk with Jesus in Galilee, as did his first disciples, but through his Holy Spirit we can shape our lives by the commands and example of his life in the Gospels. The pre-Easter life was not just some sort of prelude to the more important part centring on the cross and resurrection. It is all one in Christ. Jesus was the incarnation of the kingdom, and through the cross and resurrection we have access to that incarnation.

'What happens now?' was the exciting but challenging question of a young man I had just baptized. I told him to read one of the Gospels. He looked disappointed and told me he had done that before. I suggested he do it again, this time not to find out information about Jesus but to learn how to live a Christ-like life from Jesus. A few weeks later, he was back—alive, full of questions and overwhelming certainties, and asking why it was different now. I told him it was because, through his baptism, he was living with Jesus rather than just watching him. This young man was a rather disconcerting person to have about the place—rather like Jesus would be!

For reflection

Matthew 13 contains many parables of the kingdom. What do they say to you now?

Prayer suggestion

Pray Matthew 6:33 at the start and end of each day and notice what changes it brings about.

For discussion

Do you think the expression 'the kingdom of God' can mean the same today as it did in the time of Jesus, or should we look for a different way of describing what it means?

The outer limits of prayer

Your will be done, on earth as it is in heaven.
MATTHEW 6:10

It is Sunday morning at Manvers Street Baptist Church in Bath. Some of us travel for miles to be there; for others it is a walk around the corner. Many of us manage to come most Sundays, but, for a few of us, that is not possible, so we come when we can. We sit in our usual places, but occasionally surprise ourselves and others by moving somewhere else in the building. It has been known, on such occasions, for people to have to introduce themselves to each other, even though they have been coming to the same place of worship for years.

These days, the organ stops trying to compete with the hubbub of chat and greetings a few moments before the service begins. Someone steps forward—usually a child—and lights our candle of prayer and stillness. Gently we become less restive and silence arrives.

Then we are invited to stand to worship God, and at that moment, whether we are ready or not, whether we feel like it or not, we take leave of ourselves and embrace the fifth plea of the Disciples' Prayer: 'Your will be done.' At that moment, our tiny, brief lives with their stories of mixed fortunes, moments of bleakness and ecstasy, faith and courage, become part of the greater story of God —the story of God's aching, longing love that seeks to transform and reconcile all things to God. We cry out these words, the same words used by our Lord in Gethsemane—a cry of pastoral need and mission intensity. The fitful swirl of our own faith, always at odds with the principalities and powers of this world, embraces the grace and truth of God in Christ. These words should not be mumbled; they are the shouting, acclaiming, delighting heart of our Lord's Prayer shared with us.

In Ephesians 1, Paul describes with overwhelming delight and praise the discovery of what God is doing through Christ. His words are, in effect, an extended meditation on this part of the Disciples' Prayer. God is wisdom and has insight (v. 8). Paul believes that he and his fellow believers are in special times. They are privileged to have been born when God's wisdom and insight have brought to full view 'the mystery of his will' (v. 9). It is a plan that places Jesus Christ at the centre of all things, 'to gather up all things in him, things in heaven and things on earth' (v. 10).

Could it be that Paul had the prayer of Jesus in mind as he wrote to the Ephesian church? He knew that his letter would be read by handfuls of Christians scattered around the eastern shore of the Mediterranean. They had no great organization; there was no New Testament in their hand. Their leaders were as good as their memories of what people like Paul had told them of Jesus. They lived in a culture that was overwhelmingly dominated by the cult of the Roman Emperor. Yet, for Paul, size has nothing to do with anything. The youngest, most inexperienced convert was as much called to proclaim faith in the mystery of God's will as himself—a descendant of Abraham, a Hebrew among Hebrews, Pharisee-trained with a fantastic conversion story!

This is what we assert when we pray these words of Jesus. We place ourselves firmly among those who believe that there is a lot more going on through the action of God than we can contain within the grasp of our experience and faith. This mystery is not completely inexplicable. We cannot explain it all, but we have some experience of it. To pray 'Your will be done' is to take the focus off ourselves and seek to be caught up in the project that is greater than any of us. It is a plea, in the words of Michel Quoist, 'to rise very high and see the world the way that God does' (*Prayers of Life*, Gill & Macmillan, 1965). In fact, we do not need to rise that far. We need go no higher than the height of a cross, for that is the vantage point from which God looks at his world. It is in the glorious mystery of the cross that his plan comes to fruition and the gathering up of 'all things' has begun.

As I have mentioned before, the Baptist Union's Declaration of Principle spells out the consequences for living this part of the Disciples' Prayer: 'It is the duty of every disciple to bear personal witness to the gospel of Jesus Christ, and to take part in the evangelization of the world.' This declaration was written with the same dimensions of faith that Paul used in Ephesians. Every disciple is involved, not just some who might be more gifted or experienced. It is the world that we shape with gospel life—not just what we can see from our own doorstep.

For reflection

Read Ephesians and notice how often it reminds you of the Lord's Prayer.

Prayer suggestion

Go up to a place from which you can see much of where you live, and pray 'Your will be done, on earth as it is in heaven' in all directions and for all that you see.

For discussion

How can Christians be helped to become more confident in sharing their faith?

The prayer of the vulnerable

Give us this day our daily bread.
MATTHEW 6:11

At the beginning of the Lord's Prayer, Jesus trains our thoughts on God; he then expects his disciples to accept their own needs and vulnerability. We need sustenance: there are certain necessities without which we cannot exist. Discipleship is as much about them as a desire for God's kingdom to come and his name to be hallowed.

In this prayer, Jesus will not let us forget that we are from the dust of the earth. Our bread and our bodies have a common origin. In the praises of the psalmists we may be little less than the angels (Psalm 8:5), but in their laments we are also vulnerable and fragile creatures (Psalm 103:15–16). We may be called to sing the glories of God but we should not get above ourselves, for we all need the nourishment of God the creator (Psalm 104:14–15).

A friend once confessed that she found this request an embarrassment, because she could not get out of her mind all the millions for whom it is a vain plea. She wondered how people felt, saying this prayer in the midst of shortage, drought and famine. She wondered whether the words mocked these people as they realized that their food was available only at the whim of weather and by the action or inaction of government and NGO.

She felt that, in our consumer society with its overstocked shelves and panic-buying at the merest hint of a shortage, this call to God was profoundly odd, and she found it difficult to approach this part of the Disciples' Prayer with any sort of integrity. After all, she knew full well where her daily bread would be—at her local hypermarket with all the other things she could get on credit. She applauded the earthiness of the request, and said that she wondered whether this was the point where many people actually started praying the Lord's Prayer rather than simply saying it—but she felt like a fraud.

I think she understood the request more than she realized. We can see this when we examine the two words 'daily' and 'bread'. The Greek word used for 'daily' is a unique one, so scholars have had a field day trying to get to its meaning. Here are some of their suggestions: bread for the day, tomorrow's bread today, continual bread, sufficient, each day's bread, necessary bread. They all struggle to arrive at the same idea. In this request, we are not asking God for a guaranteed diet that comes without problem for the whole of life. We are, in fact, asking for no more than we need on a daily basis, and once again we are in the territory that Jesus explores in Matthew 6:19–21, 25–34.

Jesus calls on his disciples to rely on the daily nurture and provision of God. As a Father in heaven, God can be relied upon day by day. When we try to settle the future by our own plans and stockpiling, we move the centre of our life of faith from the creator to the created. At the heart of this prayer is a call to a daily act of trust in God, trust for today's provision. This is deeply counter-cultural. It is not an argument against careful preparation in light of the vagaries of the future, but it is a warning against trying to control the future from the present.

As for 'bread', this is meant to be a catch-all word, describing the bare necessity and also the rich variety of God's provision. It reminds us that our basic need is not luxury, and raises the question of how much we can do without. We are challenged to consider whether we have made essential what is, in fact, peripheral to our well-being.

It also tells us not to disdain the ordinary and the everyday. I may have food from the best of restaurants one day but, if it truly is the Lord's provision, the toast on the table the next day should be equally welcome.

The issue is not only about food. The Lord provides in many different ways. We are called to an incarnational faith, so our daily bread may be in the offer of a lift, the phone call of a friend, a request to pray with us, a film, a new pair of shoes, or time given to our church's outreach. Anything that nourishes what we need instead of what we want is 'daily bread'.

For reflection

Read Mark 1:16–42 and discover the different 'daily breads' offered by Jesus that day.

Prayer suggestion

Start each day with the request, 'Give us this day our daily bread', and end each day by thanking God for how the prayer has been answered.

For discussion

Do you think I have answered my friend's problem with this part of the prayer?

Prayer and forgiveness

Forgive us our trespasses as we forgive those who trespass
against us.
COMPARE MATTHEW 6:12

I have found that to preach the forgiveness of God is a most exciting and liberating experience. I have also discovered preaching our
forgiveness for each other to be a deeply demanding and painful
experience. To preach both together is what I often struggle to
do, and thus I separate what God has joined together. If I preach
only the forgiveness of God, I am in danger of selling 'cheap grace'.
When I commend the church as a community of forgiveness without
acknowledging the primacy of God's forgiveness, I burden people
with an impossible task and encourage guilt, shame and blame, for
without God's grace actively at work there can be no forgiveness
between people.

Our Lord has taken us to the deepest part of his prayer here. It is
the only part where he draws out our partnership with God. This is
a covenant moment, in which divine and human forgiveness occupy
the same space. They flow together in an eternal cycle of life-giving
power. To be forgiven is to be forgiving. The first does not occur
without the other (Matthew 18:23–35). To be forgiving is to be a
revelation of the secret work of the grace of God.

One of the great discoveries to come out of the disorder and pain
of our recent conflicts in Europe and Southern Africa has been
the wonderful connection between truth, peace, reconciliation and
forgiveness. Deep and important work has been done, and what we
now know about mediation and conflict resolution is a rich gift of
God for our age. In fact, it was always there; it is what Jesus is saying

in this part of the prayer, and his whole life was a demonstration of these words.

In Mark 2:1–12 we find a story with forgiveness at its heart. It stands at the beginning of the Gospel and acts as a template for the rest of Jesus' life. The crowds gather gladly and listen intently, but some are there to question and criticize. They fear the consequences for their faith if Jesus is given too much room. Into the centre of them all arrives a man held captive and paralysed. Healing comes when Jesus speaks words of forgiveness—and his critics rightly discern that this makes Jesus a threat. He is either a dangerous imposter or the very face of God on earth.

In his suffering on the cross, Jesus lived these words of his prayer as he looked upon his executioners and appealed to the Father to forgive them, as they were acting in ignorance. In his blunt, courageous refusal to contribute to their cycle of retaliation and violence, he both absorbed the horror of what they did and broke the chain reaction of fear and aggressive self-assertion. In that moment, the cost of divine forgiveness was seen in his peace-offering death. The face of the dying Christ became the face of God on earth.

When we pray 'Your kingdom come on earth' we are asking to see this face of Christ which is now in his people, the church, a community of the forgiven who are also the forgiving. Yet this is so hard to achieve, isn't it? One of the reasons it is so hard for me to preach of mutual forgiveness is that I know how difficult Christians can find it. It is not helpful to stand apart offering sound advice when I am not the one needing to do the forgiving. Equally, it is hard to forgive someone else when they are not ready to receive the offer.

I have heard more than one minister speak of the debilitating, even lethal effect of unrepentant Christians on their ministry. But this is not something that affects only ministers! Conflict will always occur in our churches. It is how we handle that conflict, and the consequences for future living, that make us more or less a people of the gospel.

I remember interviewing Gordon Wilson after the death of his daughter Marie in an IRA bombing. He spoke quietly and with total conviction of forgiving the people who had done it. I was filled with wonder and amazement and became completely enthralled by his extraordinary response, as he calmly explained that he was able to do it because of his total immersion in the gospel living of his local Christian community. This is what he had been taught, and when the time came, this is what he was enabled to do. Was he given a special blessing?

It is equally true that, for some people, the path to forgiveness of each other is a long journey. Geiko Muller-Fahrenholz is surely right when he writes, in *The Art of Forgiveness*, 'Forgiveness is a process whereby perpetrator and victim can set each other free to live the future in a way that the scars of the past will no longer bind or hold back' (World Council of Churches, 1997).

For reflection

Matthew 6:12 speaks of debts and debtors. How does that reshape our understanding of forgiveness?

Prayer suggestion

Pray for people you know who cannot forgive.

For discussion

Share stories that inspire you to forgive.

Prayer and temptation

Lead us not into temptation.
MATTHEW 6:13 (NIV)

In this series of reflections, I have described the Lord's Prayer as the Disciples' Prayer. In both of the Gospel versions of the prayer, it is clear that this was a prayer for his disciples to explore and use. It was more than a moment to 'close eyes and say together...' It was an offering of trust and hope to God for the way we experience life and act as followers of his Son.

I choose to use the traditional words that have been in currency in English for generations. They can sound quaint, like the phrase we are considering here, yet this strange English does highlight a difficulty that some have expressed about this petition. Would God lead us into temptation? It does not sound very helpful!

The answer is both 'yes' and 'no'. Life is full of temptations; Christian life is about responding to the leading of God. So, as we often find with the words of Jesus, we must explore more deeply and widely to discover a number of meanings in them.

God will lead us; there will be temptations on the way. God will not necessarily intervene if such moments are a time for our faith to be tested. What we are appealing for is that when such times come, we may not be tested beyond our capacity to trust and obey.

The sort of temptation that Jesus is describing in this phrase of the prayer is the kind in which we arrive at a moment of paralysing doubt that makes us feel it is too much for us and too much for God. The word 'temptation' has become a very weak word in our culture. It is used to describe the desire to eat too many cream cakes or buy too many pairs of shoes. In certain contexts, however, even these desires can become very powerful temptations, which can damage lives. Then we see how temptation can become a devastating power, an experience in which we are shaken to the core of our being.

Some translators prefer to use the phrase 'time of testing' to interpret what Jesus meant. This translation has struggled to find its way into liturgical use, but it firmly reminds us that the prayer is asking us to explore experiences of delusion and deceit, fear and compromise, when all that we hold dear asserts itself over and against the faith and discipleship of Jesus that we are embracing.

When Jesus included this petition for his disciples to use in their prayers, he was in deadly earnest because he had been there before them. The first three Gospels spell out that the temptations/testing of Jesus in the Judean wilderness were a seminal moment at the beginning of his ministry. Matthew (4:1) and Luke (4:1) speak of him being 'led' out into the wilderness to be tempted, while Mark speaks of him being 'driven' out by the Spirit (1:12). This was a God-provoked experience—Jesus was certainly led into temptation!

What happened is told in terms that evoke all sorts of echoes of the post-Passover wanderings of the people of Israel. Jesus' struggle with the devil was just what his contemporaries would have expected to happen in such a harsh, God-forsaken environment. But of course Jesus was not abandoned by God. He walked away from his baptism with the extraordinary endorsement of God deep in his heart. He is the Son of God—so what now? In the light of that calling, how should he live? What sort of life would be consistent with the affirmation of God that he has received? He tussles with the priorities of his calling with all the resources of the Spirit and word of God, and as he wrestles with these questions, we are shown a clear insight into the nature of temptation. When something is really important to us, it will contain the potential for us to distort its importance. If we believe that God has called us to a particular task or responsibility, for example, that task may well be the source of our deepest disturbance and self-criticism.

As for Jesus, so for us. God does not deliberately try to trip us up;

he longs for our obedience. But God will not create artificial, easy circumstances in which we can work out our faith. It has to be done in the real world of imperfections and difficulties. The task that we believe God has given us to do will become a test of our priorities and resolve. These days, we are encouraged to make risk assessments before we take up any enterprise. I suggest that we also need to survey the task with a temptation-assessment. (Perhaps this is the role of the spiritual leaders in a church.)

The temptations of Jesus and the experiences of the Israelites in the wilderness might start us thinking and praying as they remind us of the doubts and excuses that we might use:

- This is too difficult—let's go back.
- Let's do what other people want/attract attention to ourselves/ manipulate the results.
- We've started it—someone else can complete the task.
- This is too difficult—who can we blame?

The way to the coming of the kingdom and the doing of God's will is not easy. There are times when we are easily seduced away from a path that needs to be straight and narrow. There are also times when the path feels as if it is on the edge of a high mountain, with a sheer drop just a step away. The climb is necessary to get to the next level in the task, but the Disciples' Prayer recognizes that we may find it difficult. Jesus is quite realistic in warning his disciples that to follow him is demanding.

For reflection

Which of the temptations of Jesus are arising in your church life?

Prayer suggestion

Seek out, with God's help, the temptations hidden in the most important part of your church's mission.

For discussion

What 'times of testing' are you facing at present?

Prayer in the presence of evil

But deliver us from evil.

COMPARE MATTHEW 6:13

I suggest you read Ephesians 6:10–18 by way of introduction to this section of the prayer.

A friend has recently begun worshipping at a Catholic church. One of the features of the worship to which he has to become accustomed is the way the Lord's Prayer ends: there is no doxology. Instead, it finishes like the versions given in the Gospels, concluding with what some regard as a chilling reminder that faith in the Father, doing his will, calling for the arrival of the kingdom, receiving his forgiveness and resisting temptation will involve us in a conflict with evil.

More than once in this series of reflections, we have seen how the prayer grew out of Jesus' own experience. It was hammered out of his constant conflict with diabolical forces of disease, oppression, confusion and toxic religion. Jesus came as the great liberator. His gracious power released those whose lives had become twisted by evil spirits. He spoke words of release to those whose minds had been made rigid by cheerless religion. He fought against a political system by challenging its conventions and power.

At the synagogue in Nazareth (described in Luke 4:16–19), Jesus read from the book of Isaiah, and what he read gave him a pathway for seeking the kingdom of God. This pathway passed through the numerous encounters with people during his ministry, to Gethsemane, the cries of dereliction and achievement on the cross, and beyond the empty tomb to Paul's assertion that our struggle also is 'against the cosmic power of this present darkness' (Ephesians 6:12).

My friend tells me that as he worships among his Catholic

neighbours, he finds a positive comfort in the Lord's Prayer ending in this way. It is a powerful reminder that we leave worship to be people of light in a world shadowed by death, yet deliverance is at hand—the gift of the Lord.

Hannah Arendt, one of those who watched the trial of Nazi Adolph Eichmann, coined the phrase 'the banality of evil'. She meant by this that immense evil can be delivered by a bureaucrat who is 'simply obeying orders' and completing lists. It can emerge from a logic that seems appropriate and then takes on devilish power. It can be encountered in the posturing of a little man who triggers hatred and fear in a people's psyche. It delivers its horrid punch through being seemingly inconsequential, not to be taken seriously. Jesus noted the silly antics of those who thought to impress God by their wordy eloquence. He also poked fun at the legalism of the religious auth-orities. But there was a deeply serious reason behind his words: he knew that such behaviour had the power to deform and overwhelm.

Compassion was at the heart of the teaching and behaviour of Jesus. Where there is no compassion, there is evil. Evil is where compassion is absent. In Matthew's version of the prayer, we ask to be delivered from the 'evil one'. I take this to mean the accumulation of all the horrid, vicious, evil garbage that haunts the human race. Our unwillingness to be whom God has called us to be results in a distortion of that calling, a distortion that constantly threatens to overwhelm us.

It has been said that the devil's best piece of work is to persuade people that he doesn't exist. Maybe, but my version is that the devil is content if people ignore and ridicule him. He is feeling fine if we dress him in weirdness and spend a lot of time dwelling on his works. The last thing he wants us to do is to treat evil seriously—but in the final words of the Disciples' Prayer that is just what Jesus is doing. He makes us aware that, like him, we need to treat evil seriously and treat the liberating power of God with equal seriousness.

Evil has a personality. It can take over an individual, community or nation. Evil is what happens when a chain of events characterized by violence, despair, anger, fear and oppression progresses unheeded. Paul rarely mentions Satan or the evil one, but Romans 7:14–24 tells us that he knew what it was like to have another power fighting over his personality. In verse 25, however, he declares where he can find rescue: in Jesus Christ our Lord. Paul invested tremendous meaning and authority in each of those words.

In Jesus we see a person who has broken the cycle of evil for us. He took on the unredeemed distortion and betrayal of the shameless human race. He lived in defiance of its rotten core. His death and resurrection acted as a moment of transformation when the impact of his evil-resisting compassion was released to work in all time zones and eras. The times of powerlessness, distress and frustration will come, but, in the words of Mother Julian, 'we shall not be overcome'.

For reflection

Romans 8:18–39 describes the liberation that comes from God's deliverance in Christ.

Prayer suggestion

Pray Colossians 1:9–14 as an alternative to dwelling on evil.

For discussion

Is belief in the evil one helpful for understanding our experience of life today?

Praise and politics

For yours is the kingdom, the power and the glory.
COMPARE MATTHEW 6:13 FOOTNOTE

It is easy to forget that the New Testament could not avoid being political, written as it was against a background of Roman rule that challenged every other allegiance. As the first Christians explored their love for Jesus, they began to use descriptions that would inevitably bring them into conflict with political and religious authority. To call Jesus 'Christ' was a direct challenge to the influence of the various theologies of the Jewish faith. To call him 'Lord' was an equally confrontational challenge to the cult of the Emperor.

Although the doxology that concludes the Lord's Prayer was added many years after the time of Jesus, it is more than a piece of praise to end the prayer. As we draw our prayer to an end, we return to the one who has initiated the prayer in the first place.

Our prayer is always an answer to God. It is not our initiative; we are always the second voice in prayer. It is because God first loved us that we love God. Because God's mission is to love the world, we, as the redeemed of the world, continue the conversation in prayer that is a glad and full response to his grace and power. We should never forget our status: we are those who are responding to God, among others who have yet to make that discovery. This is the place of ultimate humility.

When we give our life to Christ, we are caught up in something far bigger than our own decision to follow Jesus. We are caught up in what some theologians call the 'Christ event'. This is what sent Paul into raptures in the opening chapters of Ephesians and Colossians, and especially in Romans 8. The work is God's; we sing the praises and then live the life that challenges every authority.

So, as we end the Disciples' Prayer, it is not just in words of praise. Along with our brothers and sisters in Christ, we are also accepting the consequences of giving our allegiance to the God and Father of the Lord Jesus. This allegiance will question and challenge all other loyalties, whether to our political system and its parties, our ecclesiastical tradition and its present form, our educational and social structures or our national identity.

I note that in the index for the Baptist collection of hymns *Praise and Worship*, 'Jesus Christ is risen today' and 'Jesus Christ is waiting' are found beside each other. The first raises our hearts in worship to the glorious worship of heaven; the second expects us to meet Jesus in the streets of the city. I wonder whether we can emphasize the former at the expense of the latter. A Christ ascended into the presence of God may have less to do with which way we vote than the risen Jesus who waits, raging, healing, dancing in the streets, but the two must go together. Christian praise is political. We raise to the heights the name that is above every name, and we cannot discern the meaning of it fully if we do not then explore and define the consequences for how we live in our society, both accepting and rejecting its conventions and cultural priorities.

In recent years, there has been a great debate over what sculpture should be placed on the fourth plinth in Trafalgar Square, which has lacked a permanent occupant since 1841. The space was filled until recently by the sculpture *Alison Lapper Pregnant* by Marc Quinn. Alison commented that she was glad to give Nelson some company. The vulnerability of her nakedness and pregnancy, as well as her disability, contrasts with the size and dimensions of other statues in the square. It invites us to ponder the nature of power, and what is the true glory in being triumphant.

The kingdom and power and glory of the Christ-like God that we celebrate as we finish our Disciples' Prayer raise the same questions for us. Where is true authority in this world? What is an authentic sign of status? What sort of glory raises our spirits and deepens our faith?

As it reaches its conclusion, the prayer asks, 'What life will you now live?' Each Sunday morning in every church there gathers a company of people who are seeking to make Jesus the centre of their life, to live close to the heartbeat of God. They seek a city not made with human hands and, when the Lord's Prayer comes alive within them, it will show.

For reflection

'To clasp hands in prayer is the beginning of an uprising against the disorder of the world' (Karl Barth). How is this true in the Lord's Prayer?

Prayer suggestion

Pray for the peace of God in the events of our world.

For discussion

What political concerns does this prayer raise for you?

Conclusion

The first readers of 1 Peter were living in a culture that kept Christians on the margins, so their lifestyle was their fundamental way of proclaiming the gospel. This did not, however, remove their responsibility to speak up for Christ when given the opportunity (1 Peter 3:15).

In this book, I have kept that responsibility in mind. I believe that Christians need to rediscover the confidence and capacity to speak clearly and bravely about what they believe and why we believe it. My reflections have been based on a series of convictions.

- We need to seek God. Shortly before he took up his post as Archbishop of Canterbury, Rowan Williams was asked what he was praying for the Church. He expressed the hope that Christians would be able to set on fire the imagination of our society with a vision of God the holy Trinity. This will not happen unless, like the psalmist, our deepest desire is to know God (Psalm 63:1–5). We have reduced our definition of belief to having a number of ideas about God, but the original meaning of the word is to give our heart to the object of our belief. To believe in God is to move into a relationship with God, one that will give energy to the task of exploring our faith with others.
- We need to be completely honest about our struggles and questioning. Jesus surrounded himself with honest people—so much so that the writer of John's Gospel constructed the core of his text around characters who were puzzled by faith and finding it difficult to cope. Smooth-browed Christian blandness is not just a turn-off; it is deceitful.
- We need to live anything that we say we believe. Jesus constantly expressed disappointment and frustration with hypocritical people. Why believe something that isn't making a difference to

the way we act? I once asked a friend what difference his conviction of having eternal life made to his daily life. He told me that it made no difference at all. Another friend, who is not a Christian, was listening to our conversation. His response was pointed: 'You Christians expect guys like me to go through the hoops to get to your God, and then you tell me it's not making no difference. Get real!' Quite.

- We need to be able to proclaim the gospel as if we were in the presence of a dying child, whether in circumstances of war, famine or persecution. I choose a child because I believe that their plight can still touch the hearts of our cynical Western culture. This means that we must explore the mystery of the suffering of God and let the good news of his love emerge from the pain of the cross. The context of the Sermon on the Mount reveals that the crowds who heard Jesus speak were coming to him primarily for healing. What he said had to ring true within sight and sound of their distress. This kind of exploration is not a popular thing to do. Too many in our culture succumb to a crass indifference to issues of justice, apart from the occasional sponsored charity event. People of the gospel cannot behave like this. The cross is the road into the heart of God, and there we must go to proclaim both vulnerability and redemption.

- We need to recognize that the gospel is an explicit challenge to all earthly authority. The Lordship of Christ has political and economic implications; we cannot shy away from these, although it is hard not to do so. We may still be trapped in a Constantinian mindset, in which we equate our culture and national identity with being Christian, as if to be British is to be Christian. This is no longer the case. Christian influence is at best patchy but certainly no longer dominant in our society, and this is both a burden and an opportunity.

Resourcing your spiritual journey

through...

- Bible reading notes
- Books for Advent & Lent
- Books for Bible study and prayer
- Books to resource those working with under 11s in school, church and at home

- Quiet days and retreats
- Training for primary teachers and children's leaders
- Godly Play
- Barnabas RE Days

For more information, visit the **brf** website at **www.brf.org.uk**